AGE OF THE CHRIST

WHERE WE ARE, THERE HE REIGNS

TOMMY GREEN

DEDICATION

Thank you Lord for establishing the work of our hands and causing us to triumph in the work of Yours—just as You have said in Your Word. I dedicate this book and my whole life to You Jesus—the One who loved me from the beginning and gave Yourself for me.

ACKNOWLEDGMENTS

Elizabeth, thank you for helping me love you the way that Christ loves the Church—it would be impossible without His grace at work in both of us. I promise to always be amazed that we are truly one.

Jed, Micah, and Bethel—the Holy Spirit has taught me more of the Father's heart through you guys than I could have learned from reading all the books in the world. I'll always remember the day each of you were born—how I lifted you in the air to the Lord, and offered you back to the One from whom you came.

And I'll always remember the day when we as a family offered up this manuscript to the Lord by lifting it in the air together to Him. Then we laid it down on the dining room table, removed our hands, and asked Him to place His hands on it.

CONTENTS

INTRODUCTION

In Christ we are the closest representation of God that the people of the world will ever see until that day when they stand before Him face to face. As the embodiment of the Lord in the earth, the whole fullness of God that infused every atom of Jesus during His earthly walk, continues to pervade every single cell of our life in Him right now.

However, the Holy Spirit is not some mystical fog floating around out in the atmosphere that surrounds people to show them the love of Jesus. Instead, He operates in and through ordinary "earthen vessels" or "jars of clay" just like you and me.

In fact, the Divine Life, Love, and Light of Jesus dwells in the Body of Christ so richly that we can say along with Him, "Anyone who has seen Me has seen the Father" (John 14:9) because "I and the Father are One" (John 10:30). As unworthy as we are, that God has actually gathered us in to His embrace and made us One with Him forever through the death and resurrection of Jesus our Lord is the deepest truth that we can ever know.

Age of the Christ

Yet we cannot afford to rest in the knowledge of simply knowing God if we intend for Him to be glorified in the greatest possible measure through our earthly lives. We're impelled by His very own Spirit within to also make Him known. Just as in the beginning Adam "knew" His wife and she conceived and brought forth a son, so we too ought to know the Lord so intimately that fruit is also born as a product of our union with Him.

Adam had a son named Cain—God had a Son named Jesus, and through Him gave birth to sons named you and me. What an amazing privilege that the Father has bestowed upon us that we should be called the sons of God by faith in Christ. But there's an even higher level of relationship with the Father that Jesus has always enjoyed, and now so do we also—the only thing better than being a son of God is being One with God.

Out of our oneness with the Lord new life emerges from us to fill the whole world with the fruit of the knowledge of His glory. He is the King of those who reign as kings and the Lord of those who rule as Lords. Just like Jesus during the days of His flesh and just like Jesus the Risen Christ of God today, ours is a rule and reign of love. If the people of the world who are not yet in relationship with God are going to taste and see that He is good, it will happen in direct proportion to the extent that they partake of His life through us.

Under the curse of our former union of nature with the race of Adam, we brought forth thorns and thistles. Now, by virtue of our union with Christ and reception of His Divine Nature through faith, we bring forth God. When we open our hearts, God comes out. When we open our eyes, God comes out. When we open our mouths, God comes out. When we open our hands, God comes out.

This book is presently the most complete statement that I can make concerning our union and communion with Father, Son, and Holy Ghost—and the fruit produced as a result. The highest ambition of my heart is that we prefer to enjoy the Presence of the Living Christ of God above anyone or anything else—infinitely beyond every other love.

Tommy Green
Lexington, KY
2010

1

IMMORTAL ORIGIN

My earliest recollections on earth are of my mother talking to me about God. I can still remember being a 3 year old boy, looking up into the sky at night and having conversations with her that went something like this:

"How big is He?"

"Bigger than the universe."

"Where did He come from?"

"He's just always been, even before all time, before the stars in the sky."

"What was He doing before He created everything?"

"Holding us in His heart."

You originated in the heart of God before ever being released into time and made to occupy space according to the will of man. Human lineage results from the embrace of mother and father, but the new creation that you are was conceived of in the embrace of God Himself and brought forth in a sovereign and supernatural act from above. You owe your birth "neither to bloods nor to the will of the flesh [that of physical impulse] nor to the will of man [that of a natural father], but to God."[1]

Your line is of God—"without father, without mother, without descent, having neither beginning of days, nor end of life; but made like unto the Son of God"[2] forever. The Christ-man has been reconstituted, and in a very real sense, although not self-existent like God Himself, we also are from everlasting to everlasting. Now because of Jesus you can say along with Him, "I came forth from the Father, and am come into the world: again, I leave the world and go to the Father."[3]

The point is this—the Father of Creation has known you from the foundation of the world and called you by name once again into the embrace from where you came. According to His design, God manifest you from His Presence into the fullness of time. In Christ "you are now *returned* unto the Shepherd and Bishop of your souls."[4]

Jesus says, "Unless you are converted and become as little children, you will by no means enter the kingdom of heaven."[5] The word "converted" literally means *reversed*. In other words, for us to enter the whole of who God is and what He makes available, we have to first stop carving our own way through life and instead place ourselves back in Him—walking on the path that He pre-arranged for us—before the world began.

Before.

Think of it. When the earth was without form and darkness hovered over the face of the great deep, you—the height and pinnacle of His creation were already in His heart. Thousands of years later, the Spirit of God brooded still—this time over your heart. The same Word which He spoke in the beginning this time resounded in your hearing and found home in the empty waste of earth that you were, which also was without form of Godliness, where darkness also infested the deep places of your being.

His Word was always alive, and now so were you. It's not so much that He spoke again, it's that the original Word never stopped being. When He first said "Let there be light," that same Word eventually resulted in you.[6] He spoke into the void of your life and swallowed it up, because His Word never returns void.

So I would look up into the stars aligned in the darkness, just like so many millions of small children before and after me, and I would say within my spirit, with groanings that are too deep for utterance, yes and amen. Children can chart with finality the breadth and length and height and depth of His great love because they have a starting point—they think that they're the center of the universe—and really they're right. Concerning those who have humbled them-selves like a little child Jesus says, "to such belongs the kingdom of God."[7]

See, pertaining to our existence, the question is not why. Not why did He do it, and not even what—as in "what was He thinking?" The real question is *who was He thinking of* when He spoke forth the stars in a single breath and appointed the entire course of heaven and earth? You. He had you in mind eternal ages ago before He ever set man in the midst of the entire realm of creation as His crowning joy. Creation itself is a sign of His providential care for you.

Psalm 139 declares that the number of God's thoughts concerning you is *infinite* in nature. His heart for you is from everlasting to everlasting. As a kid I probably had a better grasp on the concept of infinity than the most brilliant mathematician. If each star in all of creation represented just one of His reflections of me, and I could somehow peer into every untold galaxy and count them all, I still could never exhaust the sum. His thoughts toward me are more in number than can be measured with all the sands of time.

His love for us is incalculable on the one hand, and on the other we have only to look to the cross to see the truest expression of what the Spirit spoke through the Psalmist— "What is man, that You are mindful of him?"[8]

And who is He, this King of Glory, the One whose love is fixed on us? He is El-Elyon, the Most High God, the same One Who condescends to all humanity in meekness. The nations of the earth are a drop in the bucket before Him— small dust on the scales. He sits above the horizon of earth, and spreads forth the heavens. Even the highest heavens are the throne upon which He rests, and the earth itself only a stool for His feet. Yet the mind of the Lord is so full of us, and His unlimited love higher than the universe.

For our sake Jesus reveals Himself as the Alpha & Omega, but He is at once God from before A and after Z. For our sake He designates Himself as the Beginning and the End, the First and the Last, and yet He also operates outside of every known realm of order and arrangement. He Who was and is and is to come spoke and His Word continues speaking, "Before Abraham was born, I AM."[9]

Before Abraham had a single heir, God called him "father of many nations." In God's estimation his descendents were already as innumerable as the dust of the earth and the stars in the sky when as yet there were none. *Before* Levi broke the womb he paid tithes while still in the loins of his grandfather Abraham. "*Before* the mountains were brought forth, or ever You had formed the earth and the world, even from everlasting to everlasting You are God."[10]

Before.

And so it was with us already formed in His heart that Jesus "created the worlds and the reaches of space and the ages of time [He made, produced, built, operated, and arranged them in order]."[11]

Even today He "is the sole expression of the glory of God [the Light-being, the out-raying or radiance of the divine], and He is the perfect imprint and very image of [God's] nature, upholding and maintaining and guiding and propelling the universe by His mighty word of power."[12]

Newsweek recently detailed the space wars that Microsoft and Google are presently engaged in with one another. Apparently Google has developed their technology to such an extent that they can readily identify 200 million galaxies, while Microsoft lags behind, able only to view a mere 1.2 million. Imagine 200,000,000 galaxies, each like our own, the Milky Way, which contains billions of stars in itself alone.

As if that's not enough to really warp the mind, ponder this—modern science propounds that there are not millions of galaxies in the universe, not billions, and not even trillions. But that there are literally an *infinite* number of ever increasing, ever unfolding, ever expanding galaxies in the universe. Scientists can't find the edge of the universe because there is no end. (Incidentally, Microsoft has plans to unveil 2 billion more galaxies soon through its Worldwide Telescope program!) Just to give you an idea of how big a *finite* number can be, let's look at 1 trillion (1,000,000,000,000). If somehow you could count 1 million stars every day since the birth of Jesus until now, you still would not have reached 1 trillion...

If God spoke forth creation into existence during a fixed and definite season, why is the universe ever increasing, ever expanding, and ever unfolding? Because what He spoke continues to effect change here, now, and forever. When He said, "Let there be light," light never stopped being. The light shines in the darkness, and the darkness can never extinguish it.[13] Not only does the substance of what He initially spoke continue to produce substance today, but the sound of His voice continues forth through the eternity of the eternities, transforming everything in its path.

Light travels at 186,000 miles per second. Even moving at that speed, it would take literally tens of billions of years to travel the course of the *known* universe. Wherever light shines, darkness is dispelled. Sound moves much slower, but neither does it ever stop running its course, and neither does it ever stop producing change in whatever it encounters. Especially when God speaks—no Word from Him is ever without power of fulfillment. "In Him was life, and the Life was the light of men."[14] Having been born again from above by the Spirit of God, our entire being is now diffused throughout with His life, His light, and His love.

For all of the geometricians out there who need to prove it before they believe it. For those who may have forgotten or never really known to praise Him for the awesome wonder of new birth—of the great deep of His Spirit calling to the deep of ours, let me make it plain in language easily understood: His life is a line of pure Light running in either direction that eventually intersects us. He chases us down with His love, overtakes us with the blessing of His Presence, and captures our hearts forever. God inhabits eternity and He has always dwelt there with us also.

In Christ, the Ancient of Days Who holds the span of every age in His hands, has now broken forth into our world of time and space in order to satisfy the intense longing of His heart for us. Because the pain of separation caused by our sin was so grievous, He gave His one and only begotten Son so that He could gather many sons into glory in His embrace. On earth, the perfect Son Jesus "shrank from the horrors of separation from the bright presence of the Father,"[15] while the rest of humanity slinked away in darkness, perfectly content for a season with the breach in oneness.

I want to be very clear. In spirit, we descended from God into flesh and blood. Our flesh and blood stinks—no possibility of rightfully standing in the Presence of God. But thanks be to God for His unspeakable gift—Jesus Christ has freely restored our place again in the very Presence of God. The Christ of God Himself descended into man, so that we could ascend again (return) into Him.

As a 3 year old boy I thought my daddy hung the moon, and really He did. It just took me 22 more years to realize who my true Father was and is. Yet my mother was the one who in time and space revealed Him to me. She awakened me to His touch, and through awakening released me into my destiny. When she would tell me how unique and special I was, that there was none like me in all of heaven and earth, she was really telling me about the glory of God. Through those simple child-like conversations I began to know what I was meant to experience, live in, and live for—the glory of God forever.

Glory was our origination, and greater glory is our destination. We're changed into His same image from glory to glory—transfigured from one degree of being like Him to the next degree of being like Him, as we behold Him.[16] O the depth of the limitless riches of the Lord who declares that nothing can compare to "the glory that is about to be revealed to us *and* in us and for us and conferred on us!"[17]

Immortal Origin

The Lamb slain from the foundation of the world made provision for the entire course of life—our essential nature—to be converted or *reversed* from living independent of His rule and reign, to being totally dependent upon His will for us. Jesus Christ came to restore the future communion of heaven and earth shaped always and forever in His heart in the person of us.

2
BLOOD SONS

I was a missionary in the Philippines for a number of years. I went by myself in 1998 not knowing one person in the entire country, and came back in 2002 with a wife and two babies. That's a pretty successful mission trip. Mission accomplished!

Elizabeth Aquino and I were married in front of the house that we built with bamboo walls and a grass roof, high in the Cordillera mountain range in the northern part of the country. As we stood before our guests and one another at the altar of our love, we entered into a new covenant together with the Lord. In the sight of God, our marriage altar was as altars have always been—a place of offering, a place of putting to death, a place of sacrifice, a place of dying to self, a place of blood.

Jesus spoke to the Father along these lines before His own death when He said, "All [things that are] Mine are Yours, and all [things that are] Yours belong to Me."[18] The father son relationship is the most concrete expression that we have as an earthly pattern of our relationship with our Father in heaven. Likewise, there's no better tangible picture of the oneness that we share with Jesus as the Bride of Christ than the relationship that exists between husband and wife. A true father gives his entire life to his son, and a true husband does the same for his bride. As husband and wife we are heirs together of the grace of His life. As sons and daughters of God by faith in Christ, we're also joint heirs with Jesus. Both illustrations represent walking together in newness of life.

For those very reasons, the altar is also a place of new beginnings. We died on April 29 to our individual lives apart as we both said "I do—freely give myself to live only for you." New life arose that day in the midst of the setting apart of ourselves in love, and soon new life physically emerged from her—the evidence of our union—flesh of our flesh and bone of our bone. When my first child was born, the nurses brought him out to me immediately. I remember holding Jedidiah Wesley Green, the beloved of the Lord[19], in my arms for the first time. I offered him back to God with words similar to these:

"Father, this is your child. Thank you for sharing him with Elizabeth and me. As Your Word says, 'In Your love You chose Jed as Your own in Christ before the foundation of the world, and foreordained him to be adopted (revealed) as Your son.' We have no power of our own to nourish and sustain his life, so please help us draw upon You. Thank You for Your great love that You've set upon him."

My first thoughts were, "My God, how beautiful this child is. How innocent, how pure, how unblemished."

My second thoughts were just as accurate: "Yet within this boy beats the same heart that has broken the womb every time a child has ever been born into the world. At his core is a seed of life that yearns to live on his own terms, in his own time, in his own way. This boy who is now utterly dependent upon his mother and father, as perfect as he appears, will one day sit as lord on the throne of his own heart, ordering and arranging his own life."

As special as he is, my son was just like every other person when he was born. He brought nothing into the world, and he can take nothing out. The only thing that he had at birth is the one thing that he must relinquish in death—his right to be who he wants to be and do what he wants to do. Not simply yielding finally to physical death and then expecting to live again, because if a person waits that long, he has missed God forever. But renouncing himself now in favor of loving and being loved by the One who gave Himself in death so that we could live His life.

Jesus says that which is dearly prized among men is abomination in the sight of God.[20] Above all else, in our humanity we most highly exalt our right to live as we see fit—and it is exactly for that reason that Christ came to earth—to give us opportunity to die to living outside of Him. God doesn't hold us accountable for the way we were born—that would be like blaming us for having white skin or big ears. But He does judge us when we act in accordance with the nature in us that disagrees with and opposes Him.

The exercise of our own free will apart from conformity to God's will sets us at enmity against Him. It only makes sense that the one thing we were born with is also the one thing that we refuse to let go of—our right to be who we want to be and do what we want to do. Consequently, the one thing that must happen before we can enter in to right relationship again with God is the last thing that we're willing to do—surrender.

Surrender. Come out with our hands up in adoration to God alone saying, "Okay Lord, You've pursued me with your mercy and loving-kindness, overtaken me with the blessing of Your Presence, and captured my heart forever. I repent before you for carving my own way through this life that You've let me live, and I faithfully determine to place my entire being in You who loved me and gave Yourself for me."

By birth there's too much inner darkness in each one of us to come out of hiding from God in our hearts. Too much fight to remove ourselves from reigning in His place. Too much resolve to be in control. Too much of us. It's perfectly normal, and that's exactly the problem. We want what we want more than we want what God wants. In fact, to the exclusion of all else, in our natural state our whole mission in life is to realize ourselves—our own hopes, our own dreams, our own desires, our own ambition. To deny that there is a sinful root of self-interest buried within every heart is to deny Jesus Christ His reason for living and dying as a man on this earth.

At the core of humanity, deep within our marrow is a blood disease called sin. It issues forth in a million different ways, but the root is always the same—"my own life, my own way, my own terms, my own time. Me as lord on the throne of my own heart."

Jesus Christ came to extract the roots of our being, and implant the roots of His—a life totally given over to the will of the Father. In Him, our pre-disposition to sin has been excavated and His nature laid as the foundation for new life. At its root sin is wrong being that issues forth in wrong doing. Righteousness is His right being that He imparts freely which issues forth in active right doing.

We're talking here about the science of God, the exact declarations of Him Who concluded that all men are disobedient to His ways and purposes. Adam, God's only created son was originally made in the image of God. But sin came into the world because of his rebellion, and death spread to all men ever after as the result. Because all men sinned, none were able to stop its power. To the world it sounds like such a fairy tale that our first father Adam even existed—he who was constituted to enjoy the wonders of God forever in pure, unbroken fellowship.

Before God came to dwell in us, we lived with the seal of Adam's race—the sin nature—borne into our being. We were therefore, all of us who have ever drawn breath in the world, replicated in the image of and bearing the imprint of sinful man. The natural man is not created in the image of God, but reproduced through a natural process in the image of sinful man.

"O wretched man that I am! Who shall deliver me from the body of this death?"[21] Through His death and resurrection, the Christ of God destroyed the power of sin and its consequences. He abolished death, and brought forth life and immortality to light through the Gospel.[22]

> "The first man [was] from out of earth, made of dust (earthly-minded); the second Man [is] the Lord from out of heaven.
>
> Now those who are made of the dust are like him who was first made of the dust (earthly-minded); and as is [the Man] from heaven, so also [are those] who are of heaven (heavenly-minded).
>
> And just as we have borne the image [of the man] of dust, so shall we and so let us also bear the image [of the Man] of heaven."
>
> —1 Corinthians 15:47-49

In the natural realm all nations of men who live on the earth are one blood. In the Spirit, God is propagating a whole new race of men to dwell in—"a chosen race...a holy nation."[23] He's raising a family of sons and daughters according to the similitude of the only begotten Son and firstborn from the dead, Jesus. Populating the earth not with sons and daughters of a lesser rank and order, but growing us up in Christ in all things as we're conformed inwardly to His own image.

Like Jesus we were born of a woman, and because of Jesus we've been born again of the Spirit. Like Jesus we also are son of man *and* son of God. The Holy Ghost came upon us, and the power of the Most High overshadowed us, and that Holy One who was formed in us is the spotless Son of God.

"But to as many as did receive and welcome Him, He gave the authority (power, privilege, right) to become the children of God."

—John 1:12

We actually have an entirely new heredity, a new spiritual disposition, new DNA. We really are a new creation with a supernatural genetic code—and a mission from above not only to reflect the glory of the risen Lord but to completely express His nature through our character.

My son was born just like the rest of us—marked with the seal of the whole human race whose nature he inherited by birth. Just as in the natural, birth takes place at a definite point in time, so also in the Spirit, being born again happens in an instant—the life-force of God passes from Him into us.

"That which is born of the flesh is flesh; and that which is born of the Spirit is spirit."[24] When I was growing up, people would tell me all the time that I was definitely my father's son or that I looked like my brother. Just as in the natural you were born to walk like your father or look like your brother, so also in the Spirit you were born again from above to possess your true Father's heart and resemble in every respect your elder brother Jesus Christ.

As a newborn boy in the Philippines, it wasn't long before Jed Wesley Green was the new prop on my preaching tours. I would hold up my infant son and say to everyone present:

"Look at His baby hands. Look at His baby feet. The value of anything is determined by the price that someone is willing to pay, and I value this boy more than anything in the world. I would give my life for this boy. If it came down to it I might also give my life for some of you here tonight because you are truly my friends and I love you. But I would never, ever allow that which is most precious to me to have his little baby hands and his little baby feet pierced through, after having been mocked, spitted upon and tortured for you. And I would definitely not sacrifice my son so that the worst among us (who are really all of us) could live and go free. Only God has that kind of love. He not only gave his life, but He gave it for those who by nature were his enemies—you and me."

> "But God—so rich is He in His mercy! Because of and in order to satisfy the great and wonderful and intense love with which He loved us,

Even when we were dead (slain) by [our own] shortcomings and trespasses, He made us alive together in fellowship and in union with Christ; [He gave us the very life of Christ Himself, the same new life with which He quickened Him, for] it is by grace (His favor and mercy which you did not deserve) that you are saved (delivered from judgment and made partakers of Christ's salvation)."

—Ephesians 2:4-5

The Spirit of God expressly declares through the Word that once we were by nature children of God's wrath and like all mankind heirs of His indignation.[25] When I used Jed as an illustration it was a stumbling block for many to look at my beautiful baby son and understand that even though he was unadulterated that his heart life would eventually pollute him and the world through his actions.

Naturally, when we look at babies we don't see the corruption that marks humanity. But what's in the hidden man of the heart eventually comes out, revolting against the rule of God throughout the whole course of life. What's inside a person always finds expression—sin was in us, so sins came out. Now God is in us, so God comes out.

All of us are familiar with sayings such as "the apple doesn't fall far from the tree" or "children are a reflection of their parents." Jesus Himself uses great plainness of speech—"every good tree bears good fruit, but a bad tree bears bad fruit."[26] In other words—what's in the root is in the fruit.

If the roots of our being are still fixed in earth, then we're still in covenant agreement with death. But if the roots of our being are planted in His death, then we're also raised up in His resurrection life.[27]

In reference to earthly descent, God promised Abraham that the child that would issue forth from his own bowels would be his (Abraham's) own heir—that his descendents would be more in number than the dust. Speaking of heavenly seed, God also promised Abraham that the child that would come forth from his own bowels would be His (God's) own heir who would produce a line of descendents as numberless as the stars in the sky.

The Holy Spirit calls us heirs *of* God—not just having received of what is His, but having received Him. We have literally inherited God. God Himself, His Presence within us and upon us is the greatest blessing that we have ever or could ever possess. All throughout, the Word declares that we have received the Gift *of* God—not just the gifts that He gives, as if they weren't enough—but the Gift of God Himself. Jesus has sent into our lives the Promise *of* the Father. Again, not just the promised blessings that He extends and has caused us to avail of, but the Promise of Him. Christ within and among us, "the Hope of [realizing the] glory."[28]

The glory that we fell short of giving Him because we've all sinned is that same glory which we had with Him in the beginning—and it's that same glory which He will confer again. We were dead because of sin, but now we're made alive because of Jesus. God was in Christ—the Lamb slain from the foundation of the world—reconciling us to Himself before time began.

> "And [He did it] not because of anything that we have done, but because of and to further His own purpose and grace which was given us in Christ Jesus before the world began [eternal ages ago]."
>
> —2 Timothy 2:9

Just as your natural birth resulted from circumstances over which you had no control, so your rebirth resulted from His purpose and grace which He made known through the appearing of our Savior Christ Jesus. He said yes to you before the age of time, so that you eventually said yes to him.

When I stood before the altar I said yes to Elizabeth and she said yes to me. It's a great mystery that the two of us who are separate and distinct became one. She's flesh of my flesh and bone of my bone, just like the son that the Lord blessed us with.

Jesus became the answer to His own prayer—that we may be one even as He and the Father are one. God is growing us up in Christ in all things—raising a family of sons and daughters who bear His image and likeness—and thus unifying all heaven and earth.

God's chief attribute is us. Our chief attribute is God. Love for us defines Him above all else. Desire for Him marks us above all else. We are God's portion and He is ours. "In

Him we also were made [God's] heritage (portion) *and* we obtained an inheritance."[29]

In the fullness of time, Jesus the Christ of God was absolutely born, but in a larger sense He had always been, so truly He was revealed. We also were born of a woman, and born of the Holy Spirit. Biology pertains only to the sphere of this life, revelation speaks of forever—eternity past, present, and future. Forever doesn't just start now when we say "Go". Forever started forever ago. That's how long He has known us, and now in Christ that's how long we will know Him. "And this is eternal life, that they may know You, the only true God."[30]

Some years ago the television news magazine *20/20* featured a little girl with a rare blood disease. Her parents tried everything to save her life, but found that they needed a complete blood transfusion from a perfect genetic match. So in love they conceived a son and brought him forth as a substitute for her bad blood. Later when she was completely healed the reporter asked the 5 year old girl if she knew what had happened, and she did:

"My brother was born to give me his blood so that I could live."

The firstborn among many brethren left the glory of heaven with the glory of the Father which He had always had and always enjoyed, and came to inhabit the earth that we are and walk upon the earth where we are. He didn't come to live, die, and rise again just to stamp our passports to heaven so that one fine day we could appear before Him there in glory, but He did it all to deposit the life that He had—the life of heaven—in us right now. Our brother was born to give us His blood so that we could live and truly live, both now and forever,

"Blood is thicker than water" is another common saying that everyone is familiar with in reference to family ties. Yet in our human tendency to perceive truth strictly according to sense and reason, we habitually misinterpret what the Spirit expounds. The true meaning of that phrase is this—the blood we share as true brothers in Christ is more vital and intimate than even the water of the same womb that we shared as brothers in the natural realm. Our bond in Christ is more familial than any other because we're of like substance spiritually and not just of like substance biologically.

The Spirit bears witness in heaven and in earth that Jesus came by water and by blood. Jesus says, "He who eats my flesh and drinks my blood" enjoys the communion of heaven and earth. That person "has (possesses now) eternal life" and "lives in Me and I in him."[31]

Blood is an earthly representation of a heavenly reality. Even though God is Spirit, we are of the bloodline of God. Spirit is composed of heavenly substance, and that material in the earthly realm is blood. We are made of God—substantiated by His Spirit—infused with the life of heaven in the earth that we are. "The person who is united to the Lord becomes one spirit with Him."[32]

3

THE SEED OF GOD

Elizabeth and I have been blessed with three beautiful children. "The fruit of the womb is His reward"[33]—not because we're deserving, but because He is. Our children are *His* reward, not ours—He alone is worthy, and our kids belong to Him—the evidence of His glory.

God has always sought to propagate a Godly race—to raise up seed unto Himself. He created man for His glory, but Adam refused to grow into Him. He created a nation for His glory, but Israel rejected Him. Yet His plan to form a chosen race out of nothing but Himself never changed. So He gave Jesus—His one and only so that He could gather many sons to glory.

Elizabeth and I are one with one another and one with God, and our children are the outward display of that inner state of being. Anyone can look at them and see the product of our union of spirit, soul, and body. A woman can hide the fact that she's pregnant for awhile, and for a time even she doesn't know. But soon the seed of new life begins growing, and there's no longer any disguise for the nature inside—it roots down deep, grows up strong, eventually blossoms and bears fruit that appears to all. The fact that my wife and I have been together is apparent because what's inside always comes out—our children came forth to bring love, joy, and peace to the world.

Just like Jesus during His earthly sojourn, we are the visible representation of the invisible God of all creation. Fruit is borne out of our union with the Holy Spirit. The evidence of my relationship with Elizabeth Green has names—Jedidiah, Micah, & Bethel. The evidence of my relationship with the Holy Spirit has names as well—love, joy, peace, etc. All of these facets of God's nature known as the fruit of the Spirit are the proof which God within us produces—the product of His Presence.

There's a seed of everything God is in us. He engendered us of Himself. Jesus bore the cross to become the answer to His own prayer—"that they all may be one."[34] Through oneness with Father and Son, the Holy Ghost empowered us into the same union that Jesus enjoyed.

In the beginning God the Father, God the Son, and God the Holy Spirit communed as One saying, "Let Us make man in Our image, according to Our likeness."[35] He had already created the heavens and the earth and made every other form of life to bring forth new life "after their own kind." Plants yielding seed and fruit trees bearing fruit "after their own kind." Sea creatures "after their own kind." Birds "after their kind." Every living creature on earth "after their kind."[36]

But concerning man, He said essentially—"*Let Us make him according to Our own kind.*" Man was "sown a natural body" at the start of creation and now in Christ man is "raised a supernatural body."[37]

> "For just as [because of their union of nature] in Adam all people die, so also [by virtue of their union of nature] shall all in Christ be made alive."
>
> —1 Corinthians 15:22

God formed man of the dust of the ground according to the heavenly pattern of His own heart. His original plan has never changed—to the extent that life is happening in heaven, it can and should be happening in us right now. Whatever exists in the heart of God should occur in us as well.

The Lord told Moses to construct the tabernacle according to the instructions that he received on the mountain. Jesus came not only to reveal God to man—the purpose of the tabernacle; but Jesus came to put God in man—so that the tabernacle of God is with and in man. So that we become a living sanctuary. God has pitched the tent of His Presence upon us, enveloped us in glory, and overshadowed us with the cloud of Himself; but He has also come to "dwell (settle down)" and make His fixed and "permanent home" *in* us.[38]

Man was a heavenly design in the heart of God for which there was no earthly counterpart until He decided to bring him forth. When a person dies he doesn't cease to exist; neither has he never existed prior to being born. We existed in God in a pre-embryonic state until the ultimate reality came into view—Christ fully formed in us, "the Hope of [realizing the] glory."[39]

God gave the Spirit without measure to Jesus, and He'll give us that measure of His Spirit which we really want and make room for—no more, no less. We've got exactly as much of God as we truly want, but He yearns to deposit more. In His greatness He desires to multiply Himself in us.

Referring to earthly lineage God first promised Abraham, "Your descendents shall be as numberless as dust."[40] But God always means more than we think He does. When He referred to the same promise the second time He spoke of heavenly seed in saying, "Your descendents shall be as numberless as the stars in the sky."[41]

When Abraham withheld not his only son in sowing his seed of Isaac, he also sowed the Seed who is Christ. This time God, who speaks of non-existent things as though they were, restated both versions of the promise—bringing all heaven and earth together by saying, "I will multiply your descendents like the stars of the heavens and like the sand on the seashore."[42] In a figure, this was the first time that the two (heavenly and earthly seed) really became one, but the consummation of all things in Christ has always been God's plan—even before the very beginning of creation.

The Seed of God

"Making known to us the mystery (secret) of His will (of His plan, of His purpose). [And it is this:] In accordance with His good pleasure (His merciful intention) which He had previously purposed and set forth in Him,

[He planned] for the maturity of the times and the climax of the ages to unify all things and head them up and consummate them in Christ, [both] things in heaven and things on the earth."

—Ephesians 1:9-10

Earlier in his life, through the episode of Ishmael's conception and birth, Abraham unwittingly sought to breach God's plan for the future communion of heaven and earth. Fueled by his own desire for an heir, he tried to bring the promise of God to pass by and for himself. In so doing he essentially consumed his earthly seed, Ishmael—not realizing that he wasn't the promised son. "Oh that Ishmael may live before You," he besought God. If the Lord had somehow relented, Abraham would never have sown Isaac in life nor had Isaac to sow in death. Ishmael required no faith. Isaac required a death.

Many years after the birth of Isaac, God realized for us an even fuller dimension of the promise when Abraham learned to plant his (His) heavenly seed (Seed) Isaac (Christ). When Abraham first heard the voice of God saying, "Take now your son, your only son Isaac, whom you love"[43] and offer him up, Isaac was as good as dead—the sacrifice was already complete in Abraham before he ever lifted the blade. Even though the Lord stopped him from following through while the knife was in mid air, God gave life to and from the dead in that the father figuratively received his only son back from the grave.

God still gives life to the dead right now...and for-ever—"The hour is coming and now is when the dead will hear the voice of the Son of God, and those who hear will live."[44] God is ever in the process of fulfilling His promise, always performing that which He has spoken— *"The time is coming and now is..."*

Isaac resulted from the earthly seed that was sown when Abraham got Sarah pregnant. Christ resulted from the heavenly seed that was sown when Abraham sowed Isaac in death. The way for a seed to die is not to eat it—it then perishes with the using. The way for a seed to die is to plant it. The way to Life is through death. Ishmael perishes with the using, Isaac lives forevermore.

Seedtime and harvest endure forever. They refer to yielding and bearing. When we yield the seed of our human nature and subject it to the death of Jesus, we bear the image of God as the result.

"Always carrying about in the body the liability and exposure to the same putting to death that the Lord Jesus suffered, so that the [resurrection] life of Jesus also may be shown forth by and in our bodies."

—2 Corinthians 4:10

30

If we want to experience the power of a new life lived for Him, we have also to share in the same exposure to death that He subjected Himself to even while in the body. In conformity to His death, we attain unto the resurrection from the dead that lifts us into Him even while still in the body.

I remember the season when I had first surrendered to the Lord. I had been tending a garden in the back yard of the house where I was living. In a dream Jesus woke me in the middle of the night, took me outside, and pulled back a huge swath of earth. Underneath, I was dead, and yet I was alive with Him as we continued walking together. The Lord sowed me in the earth, and raised me into His life.

Speaking of His own life and death Jesus said, "Except a corn of wheat fall into the ground and die, it abideth alone."[45] His external reality mirrored His inward state of being. To live like Jesus, we have to die like Jesus. The cross that He bore in death was the same one that He carried all throughout life—it just became visible at Calvary. He constantly lived a life of "not My will, but Yours be done", and He died the same way. We've been planted together in the likeness of His death so that we may also be planted together in the likeness of His resurrection.[46]

Christ lives in us in the fullest possible measure through deeper death. His Kingdom is the reverse of everything the world treasures and values. The way up is down. He must increase, and He does through us. We've been immersed into His death, so that we may be immersed in His life. We've become one with Him by sharing a death like His, so that we're also one with Him in sharing a life like His. For us, death has been swallowed up in victory because we're consumed by Him.

When people get hungry apart from faith they eat their seed. As evidenced by the episode with Ishmael, Abraham wanted to consume the promise for himself. But God kept reminding him of the dust of the earth and the stars in the sky, and he kept visualizing the harvest.

Obviously, it wasn't easy for a 99 year old man to look at his 90 year old wife and believe that God was going to give him an heir from his own bowels. Yet he "considered not his own body now dead, being about an hundred years old; neither yet the deadness of Sarah's womb. But he grew strong and was empowered by faith, as he gave glory to God. Fully persuaded that what He had promised he was able also to perform."[47]

He wasn't looking at the impossibilities. He had entered the season of the deadness of not only Sarah's womb, but his own too—his inability to conceive and bring forth—and yet he was fully persuaded.

Faith determines what you see. What you see determines what you sow. What you sow determines what you reap.

Who's responsible for our outflow, us or God? When I got my wife pregnant I was responsible. I sowed the seed, not God. Yes, He gives seed to the sower, and yes He also gives bread to the eater—or, the increase. But if I'm responsible for the outflow, then why wouldn't I also be responsible for the intake? In other words, if I only sow 1 tomato plant during the spring, God isn't the reason why I didn't reap 10 tomato plants during harvest.

If we want to live like Jesus, then we need to die like Jesus. Harvest is directly proportionate to seedtime—in other words, you reap what you sow. Your external reality is determined by your inner state of being. Plant your self— the man of dust—deeper in His death so that Jesus—the Man of Heaven—will arise in the earth.

Regarding Ishmael, God promised Abraham that He would make of him a great nation. Regarding Isaac, God promised Abraham that through him *all* the nations of the earth would be blessed. Jesus is that seed of God and seed of man through whom all the nations of the earth are blessed—He is the Sovereign of Ages and King of the Nations. Jesus the Son of Man and Son of God was slain and has redeemed us to God, by His blood out of every tribe and tongue and people and nation.

My kids receive their education at an elementary school with a global studies emphasis. Children not only attend from many different nations, but they spend a significant amount of time learning about the cultural heritage of the world. As I was dropping them off at school one day I found myself repeating the promise to them that God had spoken to Abraham concerning Christ—"In you all the nations of the earth are blessed."[48]

Because the Seed of Christ is in us, in us all the nations of the earth are blessed. Ordinary as we are, we house the glory of God. So that the excellency of the power is shown to be of God and not of us, the treasure of Jesus Christ—His divine life and divine light is found in the "earthen vessels" or "jars of clay" that we are.[49]

The Holy Spirit is not some mysterious fog floating around out in the atmosphere whacking people on the head and saying, "Here's Jesus." He's operating in regular people—revealing Himself through us.

The testimony of the Father concerning His children is the same as He had and has for His only begotten Son Jesus—"This is My beloved son, in whom I am well pleased."[50] The world looks upon us and sees according to its own system of being and doing—Jew or Gentile, uncircumcised or circumcised, black or white, American or Asian, male or female. But God looks on the hidden man of the heart and sees the life of His Son Jesus.

Faith closes the distance between what God sees and what we see. When preaching I have often held up an apple seed and asked people what they see. Nearly everyone has always answered, "a seed." A perfectly natural response in the realm of sense and reason.

But faith sees the supernatural—not only a seed but an apple. Not only an apple but a tree with lots of apples. Not only a tree with apples on it, but a whole orchard. Within the power of that one seed is the power to produce a world full of fruit.

The Seed of God

There's a seed of everything God is in us. The same DNA that's in the seed is in the apple, and in the tree, and in the orchard. Jesus says that the Kingdom of God is like the least of all seeds, which when it is sown, produces the greatest of all trees. The soil of the heart reveals the kind of seed that's been sown and creates a harvest accordingly.

What He engenders in us though is not only meant for us, but so that others can eat and be nourished by His life. Abraham learned this truth the hard way. In clinging to Isaac, his desire to hang onto his promise with all his might would have cost the rest of the world the light of Jesus Christ had God not intervened to sever the hold at its root.

Where the Spirit is Lord, there is freedom. The seed of God's Presence roots down deep in the heart, grows up strong, blossoms and bears fruit for the liberty of all. How could He cultivate anything less than perfect freedom? He only gives of who He is—not of who He's not. A Godly source leads to Godly growth—what's in the root is in the fruit.

What most of us perceive as a total deficiency God sees as a lack of development. Just as the human body is composed of the same chemical elements that are found in earth, so also the essential elements of Christ comprise the hidden man of the heart. For that reason, it's not exactly accurate to say things like, "I just don't have any peace or I just don't have any patience."

No matter what your present circumstances look like on the outside, you do have the fruit of the Spirit on the inside, if only in seed form. It may be present in someone else in ready to eat form, and in another as a whole orchard—while in you visible fruit still hasn't materialized. But because God lives in you, all of the ingredients of Christ are a present reality, even if fruit hasn't yet been brought forth unto perfection.

Faith determines what you see. What you see determines what you sow. What you sow determines what you reap.

Visit any garden center and notice how seeds are packaged for sale. The picture on the front of the packet isn't the seeds—it's a snapshot of the harvest. Taking a picture of a bunch of seeds isn't going to sell any seeds. But a picture of the harvest produces the harvest in your heart in advance, and by faith God actuates it into existence for all to partake of as a result.

Just like Jesus we also are the word made flesh and dwelling among the people that God places around us. When Philip said "Lord show us the Father and that is sufficient for us," Jesus upbraided him with His response— "Philip, have I been with you such a long time and still you do not know and recognize Me? Anyone who has seen Me has seen the Father."[51]

Since we bear witness to the life of Jesus, "Anyone who has seen Me has seen the Father" should be our testimony also. We're one with God in thought, purpose, and action and one with Him in spirit, soul, and body. We too are the

Word made flesh and dwelling among the people of the world—a living epistle known and read by all[52]—a people who require the words of His mouth more than life itself.

"The testimony of Jesus is the spirit of prophecy."[53] The true sayings of God—the exact declarations contained in His Word—belong to us to express. Prophesy is for comfort, for consolation, for edification, for encouragement. When we communicate the Father's heart through His Word we're turning loose the greatest power in the entire universe. The love of God runs a course that carves its way like a mighty river through the hardest hearts, breaking down all resistance in its path.

The Word of God says, "Where the word of a king is, there is power."[54] The Word of the King of Glory dwells in us. When we broadcast the seed of that Word residing in our hearts, a harvest of righteousness is produced. We should always look for tangible fruit, but just because we might not be around to see it, doesn't mean it isn't so. As it is written, "I have planted, Apollos watered, but God gave the increase."[55]

If I were to guess, in the context of my recovery ministry, out of every 99 men that I attempt to sow into who have no relationship with Jesus, maybe 1 becomes fruitful by fully surrendering to the Lord. Sometimes when I'm worshipping alone with my guitar I sing (usually when I'm lacking visible proof that I'm doing any good and maybe even feeling a little sorry for myself) the song of Habakkuk:

"Although the fig tree shall not blossom, neither shall fruit be in the vines; the labour of the olive shall fail, and the fields shall yield no meat; the flock shall be cut off from the fold, and there shall be no herd in the stalls:

Yet I will rejoice in the LORD, I will joy in the God of my salvation."

—Habakkuk 3:17-18 KJV

In terms of producing visible and lasting fruit, whether I see results or not, I praise the Lord for the awesome opportunity to publish His goodness, and rest in the knowledge that it's up to Him to move in the hearts of men. It's God who fixes the new heavens as a tabernacle and lays the foundation of a new earth—it's the work of the Lord to save men, infusing the dirt that we are with new life from above. I only faithfully attest to Jesus in bearing His testimony forth as an eyewitness to His majesty.

I'm not saying that we shouldn't enjoy success in ministry, just that too often we hold a view that's contrary to the will of God when it comes to fruitfulness in our own lives. We confuse bringing forth fruit unto perfection with actual perfection. And because we don't accurately understand what the Presence of God is upon us for, we don't now see the results for which God longs.

The Anointed One is in me for me—as comforter, counselor, advocate, intercessor, strengthener, helper, standby.[56] But the Anointing is upon me for other people—so that they can taste and see that the Lord is good.

The Seed of God

Once I was praying on the floor of my bedroom when I heard in my spirit a distinct impression of the Lord saying, "Do you see that picture on your wall?" I have an antique print of fruit spilling over the sides of a bowl—the kind you might have found hanging in your great-grandmother's house. I like it because to me it represents the fruit of the Spirit.

I said, "Yes Lord, I see it."

He replied, "Do you know what it would look like if I had painted it?"

"No Lord."

"Apple cores. Grape stems. Orange rinds. Banana peels."

Like the disciples during Jesus' day, I didn't get it. So I felt as though He explained:

"The fruit that My Presence within you produces is not meant just so that you can live a perfectly waxed, perfectly polished, perfectly well-rounded, perfectly proportioned Christian life.

"What I produce in and through you is for others to eat and be satisfied. My life should flow out of you in mighty torrents of love, refreshing everyone with whom you come in contact. The fruit of My Spirit is meant for the nourishment of the world. Not for you to live some full-orbed life that's always just out of reach for others to enjoy.

"How is the world going to taste and see that I am good except they partake of Me in you?

"My love is better than wine, but I don't produce it apart from squeezing the fruit of My life from you."

None of us like to be squeezed, and no one likes to be broken. I learned this truth of God while on the mission field overseas. The Philippines is dotted in every village throughout the entire country with bakeries that produce very inexpensive bread—inexpensive relative to American standards. One of my favorite things was to buy 50 or so pieces and distribute it to the multitudes of little boys and girls who otherwise didn't have the fraction of a cent to buy it for themselves.

I often noted how beautiful the assortments of bread looked behind the glass, and was struck more than once with the thought of how frustrating it must be for hungry children to pass by knowing that they couldn't afford just one piece. God reminded me also more than once, that the Church is very much engaged in the business of the world—producing substance which is indigestible to people in desperate need.

We are fresh bread in the house of God—the bread of His Presence, but we're spoiled inside because we won't let God break us. We're so drunk on the wine of this world that He who saves the best for now can't even pour Himself out so that others can taste the wine of His love.

The religious people of Jesus day reproached Him for allowing His disciples to pick the standing grain and eat it when they had nothing else. He replied, "Have you never read what David and his men did when they were hungry? How they ate of the showbread that wasn't lawful for them to partake of."[57]

The Seed of God

Like the rest of us, I've been guilty of putting on a show with the Presence of God by hoarding Him all for myself. I've been the showbread that no one but a few religious people could eat—choked with the cares of this life and washing them down with the wine of this world. When all along He has wanted to take us, ordinary as we are—just a few small fish and a couple pieces of bread—and bless us by breaking us and distribute us to multitudes of men, women, and children. Whether they realize it or not, the world is famished for the fresh bread of His Presence and thirsty for the wine of His love.

Jesus won't partake of the juice of the grape until He drinks it new in the kingdom of God. The kingdom of God is righteousness, peace, and joy in the Holy Ghost and the Holy Ghost is in you. Having been made a partaker of the divine nature, now it's your turn to be partaken of by the people that He places around you each day. You may be nothing more than a little boy's lunch, but there is a seed of everything God is in you.

Jesus Christ came in the flesh, and He's coming again in the same way that He left. But right now He's in the flesh in you. When God looks at you He sees Himself—or wants to at least. "From this point on we know no man according to the flesh,"[58] says the Spirit of the Lord through Paul. I'm not saying that God doesn't see your imperfection—only that in love He has judged it already in Christ. When He looks upon your life, His testimony concerning you is the same as

He had for Jesus—"This is My beloved Son, in whom I am well pleased."[59]

Jesus became the answer to His own prayer. We are one with God and one with one another. You are the house of God and He is the bread inside, and out of your innermost being flows the love of His life.

"You give them something to eat."[60]

4

KINGDOM WITHIN, KINGDOM WITHOUT

We need to show the world who Jesus is, instead of allowing the world to show us who He isn't. The world around us is a picture of what's in the hearts of men. The substance of your external life is composed of what you possess inwardly. If God is in you, God will manifest Himself all around you.

One of the congregations that I helped establish overseas was a fellowship inside a maximum security prison. Out of 265 inmates, I pastored roughly 40 men on a weekly basis—Sunday services, counseling sessions throughout the week, ministering to their families in the villages where they where from, etc.

During the first outreach that I conducted we noticed an 8 year old little girl named Maybelle who was actually living inside the prison. Obviously if a child is living there, jail is not like we know it to be here in America. No one, including violent offenders, is locked down in a cell; but instead prison is like free flowing community within the confines of the walls. Inmates cook their own food, sleep inside or outside as they choose, play basketball in the yard, and basically do whatever they want.

Maybelle's daddy was incarcerated on drug charges and her grandmother was locked up in the women's facilities which were located on the upper level. She had no other family, so the provincial warden was allowing her to live in the midst of some of the most black-hearted criminals in the country. Although her father was loving and protective, we suspected and later confirmed that Maybelle had endured unspeakable suffering at the hands of some of the other inmates.

Our ministry operates a children's home, and we immediately gathered her up and led her out to a life of peace and safety. This is Church for us. The Lord has charged His Body to rescue and recover the children that the world throws away like so much trash. In one single moment in time, Maybelle went from hopeless to Jesus.

> "[The Father] has delivered and drawn us to Himself out of the control and the dominion of darkness and has transferred us into the kingdom of the Son of His love."
>
> —Colossians 1:13

We're called to translate darkness into light. Our hearts should be filled with those who have been robbed of life.

Sadly, many other churches and ministry groups knew about Maybelle and did nothing. Unbelievable. Just like the man who questioned Jesus, our tendency is to justify our inaction, and so we also ask "Who is my neighbor?"

> "And Jesus answering said, A certain man went down from Jerusalem to Jericho, and fell among thieves, which stripped him of his raiment, and wounded him, and departed, leaving him half dead.
>
> And by chance there came down a certain priest that way: and when he saw him, he passed by on the other side.
>
> And likewise a Levite, when he was at the place, came and looked on him, and passed by on the other side. But a certain Samaritan, as he journeyed, came where he was: and when he saw him, he had compassion on him,
>
> And went to him, and bound up his wounds, pouring in oil and wine, and set him on his own beast, and brought him to an inn, and took care of him."
>
> —Luke 10:30-34 KJV

Yet truly we all at more than one point in time have "passed by on the other side" of a world that is dying for abundant life. Instead of binding up the wounded—pouring in the oil of His Presence and applying the wine of His blood, we have all gone about our own lives without showing the love of God. The Father who set us on His own burden bearer Jesus, wants us to care for others just like we do for ourselves.

Age of the Christ

Everywhere I minister people invariably ask some version of this question—"Why don't we see God move the way we know He wants to?" We all spend time searching His heart for the obvious answer: God manifests Himself in the world around you in direct proportion to the extent that He reigns in you. In fact, the Holy Spirit in you flows out of you to define the world around you. We're called to demonstrate the reality of heaven in the earth which we are, and upon the earth where we are. His kingdom has to come in the earth that you are before His will is ever done on the earth where you are.

> "The first man [was] from out of earth, made of dust (earthly-minded); the second Man [is] the Lord from out of heaven.
>
> Now those who are made of the dust are like him who was first made of the dust (earthly-minded); and as is [the Man] from heaven, so also [are those] who are of heaven (heavenly-minded).
>
> And just as we have borne the image [of the man] of dust, so shall we and so let us also bear the image [of the Man] of heaven."
>
> —1 Corinthians 15:47-49

Not only do we "groan inwardly as we wait eagerly" but "the whole of creation waits in eager expectation" for the sons of God to manifest Christ in the earth.[61] The kingdoms of this world become the kingdoms of our Lord as a result of His life in us issuing forth from us. He shapes your heart

46

life and by virtue of that inward conformity to the image of Jesus Christ, you shape the world around you accordingly. The Kingdom of God is not only about deep, heart transformation, but the transformation of place as well.

I have a friend who the Lord rescued dramatically—just like He has for all of us who are called by His Name. God reached down into the toilet bowl of her life and drew her up out of the filth—out of the miry clay, and founded her on the Rock Who is Jesus Christ. He alone established her goings, and put a new song in her mouth, even a song of praise to our God.

When she was saved and quit being a thief and a drug user among other things, her whole world began to change—literally. God awakened in her the destiny that He had already prescribed from the foundation of the world, and she began to develop His heart for the broken and vulnerable. Today she operates a recovery ministry to the homeless, poor, and addicted called *The Lighthouse*. The facilities stand on grounds that once harbored every form of immorality. Because of what God did in the heart of this one woman, today the same city block that used to be given over to evil now belongs to the Kingdom of heaven..

In Christ, we're a sovereign state. Where we are, there He reigns.

Because we've received in our hearts a kingdom that's not of this world, and we want others to experience that same love, the life of God all around us begins to emerge.

As ambassadors of Christ, we're from above, sent to colonize the earth below—called to live the life of up there down here. Though we live within the confines of flesh, blood, and earth, we're filled with and controlled by the Spirit of God.

Jesus spent the entire substance of all that He had—spirit, soul, and body—in order to give God opportunity to fully form His life in the hearts of men by recreating them in His own image. During Jesus' earthly walk, God's order was exemplified for us all: the body is subject to the soul, the soul is subject to the spirit, the spirit is subject to the Spirit of God. When spirit, soul, and body are arranged according to the rule of God, He establishes His reign wherever we are. The kingdom within becomes the kingdom without— His domain issues forth all around.

"The kingdom of God is like leaven which a woman took and hid in three measures of meal until the whole was leavened."[62] If we want the yeast of God to arise in our midst, we need to make room for His life to increase within.

The kingdom of darkness operates on the same principles, just in reverse—"a little leaven leavens the whole lump."[63] When the bodily life exercises authority over the spirit, or when the soulish realm of sense and reason rise up to a place of preeminence, then disorder manifests all around as a result.

I have another friend whose dwelling place is a health hazard because her own house she hasn't kept spiritually speaking. Inside, the generational junk of the ages—all manner of clutter and chaos—is stored up in every corner. She refuses to let the light of God illuminate her heart, so she also refuses to let the light come in through the windows of her house. Her physical dwelling place is falling down all around from decades of neglect because she won't let Jesus work in her life. As a result, her spiritual dwelling place is falling down all around her as well—her bones and hair are brittle and broken, her skin is sallow and her eyes hollow and sunken. What's visible on the outside is just a snapshot of what's going on inside.

Our external reality is a reflection of our internal state of being. Health in every form is perfect balance between what's going on inside and what's happening in the atmosphere outside. Sickness is just the opposite—external forces ravaging the inward life. In Proverbs 13:17 the Amplified Bible says, "A faithful ambassador brings healing." The King James Version simply says, "a faithful ambassador is health."

We represent the Most High whose business is the same as it has always been—rescue and recovery. We lay hold of people by force because of the treasure that they are in the sight of the Lord. "By word and deed, we…aim to bring others into harmony with God"[64] whose love is the most unstoppable power of all.

There's no defense against the love of God—it's the greatest force in the entire universe. The love of God flows like a river, carving through the walls of the hardest hearts, breaking down every form of resistance involved. God's love never fails to violently oppose all that oppose Him by opposing themselves.

> "And the servant of the Lord must not strive; but be gentle unto all men, apt to teach, patient,
>
> In meekness instructing those that oppose themselves; if God peradventure will give them repentance to the acknowledging of the truth;
>
> And that they may recover themselves out of the snare of the devil, who are taken captive by him at his will."
>
> —2 Timothy 2:24-26 KJV

The kingdom of heaven endures violent assault today. As the enemy tries to prevail, the people of God seek to further extend His reign. There is no violence in heaven—the suffering is in the earth right now. His kingdom is not of this world, but His kingdom comes to occupy the world and eventually trans-figure the entire realm of creation. When Jesus walked on the earth, there was no violence where He was from, only where He was. He came to put His life in us so that His Presence would manifest from us to transfigure the world.

> "And from the days of John the Baptist until the present time, the kingdom of heaven has endured violent assault, and violent men seize it by force [as a precious prize--a share in the heavenly kingdom is sought with most ardent zeal and intense exertion]."
>
> —Matthew 11:12

Kingdom Within, Kingdom Without

Rogelio is an orphan who was born with severe mental and physical impediments. When we found him he couldn't even walk anymore because he was living all day in a space about the size of a half bathroom. He was starving—literally and for affection. His older brother was supposed to take care of him, but he was severely neglected instead—left in soiled clothes for days, and never taken outside for fresh air and sunshine.

We immediately brought him out of the prison of his circumstances, and became moms and dads, brothers and sisters to him. The first meal that he had with us upon arriving at the children's home was a great big bucket of spaghetti—he ate the whole thing and was ready for more.

Hear the voice of the Lord concerning true shepherding: "I will seek that which was lost and bring back that which has strayed, and I will bandage the hurt and the crippled and will strengthen the weak and the sick."[65]

Today, Rogelio is empowered by the joy of the Lord. He can even walk! But the greatest part of all is the love of Jesus that he received. The Lord has made us living signs and wonders that point the way to Him and show His glory to others.

A miracle is by definition a visible interruption of the laws of nature. Jesus took upon Himself the nature of men in order to take the nature of men out of them. There's no greater miracle than the new creation that we are. Now instead of what we were born with, we have the Holy Spirit

51

as a down payment of our full inheritance. Our co-mission along with God is to place that life in others as a deposit of even greater glory.

Jesus constantly released the life of heaven that He had always enjoyed before coming to inhabit flesh and blood. What existed there He came to bring here, and so He teaches us to pray that our present reality become "as in heaven, so in earth."[66] Through the power of the Holy Ghost, He lived here to show forth the Presence of God that He had there. Jesus didn't come to live some kind of super-Christian life that's always just out of reach for the rest of us to enjoy. He came here as the Son of God to save us from our sin but lived as the Son of Man to show us what's possible through Him—a life of complete dependence and entire submission to the Father.

The people of God are called to model the ordinary affairs of heaven. His life and nothing else is our standard. We're empowered to live just like Jesus by the same Holy Spirit Who empowered Him— "as He is, so are we in this world."[67] The life that He lived when He walked on earth as a man is the same life that He continues living right now. The life of heaven is only a breath away, and it ought not to be so. The life of heaven should be the breath that we breathe and the life that we live—right now. Heaven has broken forth into the earth that we are, and consequently must be made manifest on the earth where we walk.

In death the Lord took upon Himself everything that was not allowed in heaven. He carried the weight of all humanity's sin with the consequences in His own body on the tree. The cross that Jesus bore in death was the same one that He carried all throughout life—it just became visible at Calvary. The kingdom within—"not my will but yours be done"—became the kingdom without, for all the world to avail of.

Jesus became the curse for us, so that we could not only receive His life but so that we could minister Him to others as well. Under the curse of sin we brought forth thorns and thistles—in Christ we bring forth God. When you open your mouth, God comes out. When you open your hands, God comes out. When you open your eyes, God comes out. When you open your heart, God comes out. When God reigns in you, the King's dominion within becomes the King's domain without.

In life and in death Jesus always sought to show forth the perspective of the Father in heaven, and for this He was violently opposed, and so will we be also. But in love we too seek to demolish and overthrow every force in opposition to our God. Like Jesus, we use the authority given to us to undo the work of the enemy and release the captives into their destinies.

By faith Jesus could foresee the breakthrough that would occur in the Decapolis region. When He said, "Let's go over to the other side,"[68] He must have known what awaited Him there, and so He had some idea of what it would take to get across. And yet it was a beautiful day and He needed rest, so He laid down on a pillow in the stern of the vessel and slept as they headed across the sea. Suddenly a great storm arose, and the wind and the waves threatened to capsize the boat. The disciples were "sore afraid" so they went down into the inner chambers and awakened Jesus.

As we all know, He came and stood near the front of the boat and spoke to the wind and the waves saying, "Peace, be still." Just as suddenly as the storm arose, "the wind ceased, and there was a great calm." What was in Him came out of Him to define the world around Him. Then He upbraided the disciples for their lack of faith: "Why are you so timid and fearful? How is it that you have no faith (no firmly relying trust)?"[69]

And they all marveled saying "What manner of man is this, that even the elements obey Him?"[70] He's the same manner of man as us. Sons of God rightly related to the Father in Heaven. The Church of Jesus Christ is the visible representation of the invisible God of all creation—the embodiment of the Lord of heaven and earth.

We're the same manner of man as Jesus was and is. Your life is an open heaven wherein the people of the world look to behold the glory of the Lord. Go down into the inner chambers of your heart and let the God-man arise in the earth. Awaken the Christ in you to quiet the rage of human life, and still the forces of darkness arrayed against God.

Jesus said to Peter, and by extension He says to us today, "I will give you the keys of the kingdom of heaven; and whatever you bind (declare to be improper and unlawful) on earth must be what is already bound in heaven; and whatever you loose (declare lawful) on earth must be what is already loosed in heaven"[71] We're called to cancel the operation of the enemy in the earth and release the life of heaven for the world to enjoy.

The Church cannot afford to go about the Father's business the same way that we always have. Peter saw the miracles—even described himself as an eyewitness to the majesty. He did it all with Jesus. Walked on water with the Man, watched His countenance transfigured on the mount, saw Him alive from the dead—even received the Holy Ghost from the breath of His own mouth as He spoke these words, "As the Father has sent Me, I also send you."[72]

It only makes sense that someone with that kind of history in the Presence of God would be ready to take the world for Jesus. But after all of this—all of the kingdom and the power and the glory—the best that Peter could manage to come up with was, "I'm going fishing." And the other disciples said the same—"We're going with you."[73]

Can you imagine? At the same time that the *Risen* Christ of God still walked the earth as a man, after charging His followers with a commission to operate just as He did, that they essentially said to themselves, "I don't really know what to do, so I'll just do what I've always done—let's go fishing."

Through His resurrection, Jesus spoiled the power of sin, death and hell, and then He walked through *closed* doors to give the same authority to them, imparting the peace of the kingdom each time that He did. "Peace be unto you," He said three times in showing Himself alive—and He meant for them to go about the Father's business with no limits as well—opening and closing, binding and loosing, stewarding and releasing the kingdom of God—the same kingdom to which He gave them the keys. And the best response that they could muster up was to go fishing?

Yeah, I can imagine because just like the Church I'm still doing much of the same stuff that I've always done in exactly the same fashion that I've always done it. Falling back on human ingenuity, education, training, and intellect—drowning in the sea of my own inability to engineer the right results when all along Christ is walking peacefully on the shore of my life having already prepared a meal. And just like Peter, the outcomes are the same for all of us—toiling all night for nothing.

Then at the sound of His voice we recognize Him for who He is, and just like Peter later on, the closed doors in *our* lives start opening with no effort on our part. Suddenly we find ourselves all in—cutting every cord that kept us safely moored in the harbor, having launched out into the deep—even jumping overboard to get to Him, dragging a net with more abundance than we can possibly draw in.

The same Holy Ghost who indwelt Jesus dwells in us. We don't have a lesser Spirit to rely upon than He had. The power that the Father exerted in raising Christ from the dead is here present in us right now.

If we follow Him, He will make us fishers of men.

5
BETTER COVENANT, BETTER PROMISES

In order to create for Himself a people like no other, God entered in to agreement with Abraham to establish the Jewish race. Out of nothing but a promise, He formed a people who were no people and called them forth to possess a land which wasn't their land. Much later on, because they eventually refused to recognize Yeshua as the Messiah, they failed to apprehend the fullness of what God had in mind.

Under the old covenant the provision was set aside—all they had to do was enter in. Under the new covenant the Provider is placed inside—all we have to do is invite Him in.

By giving God the place of Lordship in our lives, we become joint heirs together with Christ. Not only of all that is His, but of all that He is—wealth which no man could otherwise experience—except by saying yes to Him.

In receiving the Lord we become One—flesh of His flesh and blood of His blood. "He who feeds on My flesh and drinks My blood dwells continually in Me, and I [in like manner dwell continually] in him."[74]

Blood is the great miracle of human life. The blood of Jesus is the greatest miracle of all time. Among other functions, blood supplies oxygen on a cellular level, carries nutrients throughout the body, and expels contaminants. Though produced at the core of who we are, not even scientists can fully describe how blood forms in the marrow of our bones.

The blood of our Lord operates along the same lines—supplying breath for every cell of our being, nourishing us with His very own life, and vanquishing every trace of the enemy. By the blood of Jesus, the Lord God has become the core of who we are.

God originally created man to share one common blood. Through the sin of the first man Adam, death entered into the world to infect every one ever born. Through the cleansing blood of Jesus, God provided a new and living way to enjoy all that He made ready for those who love Him.

Abraham lived between Adam and Jesus to foreshadow the future which God had already forged in advance. The Lord cut a covenant with him for the Hebrew nation and later the Messiah to arise from nothing but the loins of this one old man. "Human reason for hope being gone"[75], Abraham trusted in the Word of God and hoped in faith that he should become the father of many nations, just as he had been promised.

Better Covenant, Better Promises

This 99 year old man who had no heir was already as good as dead when his 90 year old wife conceived a son whose line would beget the Seed of God. Their agreement was ratified by a blood sacrifice to show forth in a type the Self-Existent One—Jesus Christ—the Lamb slain from the foundation of the world.

The covenant that God established with Abraham had a three fold approach which extended a promised land, a promised son who would continue Abraham's earthly line, and a Promised One who would form a new creation of men. God swore by Himself saying to Abraham—"to your seed I will give this land" and "so numberless shall your descendants be" that "in you all the families of the earth shall be blessed."[76]

Although Abraham never stepped foot in the promised land nor saw the Promised One who would descend from him to bless the world, he remained fully persuaded that what God had promised He was able also to perform.[77] Abraham believed God, and for that reason alone he was declared righteous in the sight of the Lord.

The Christ of God came down through the ages by the bloodline of Abraham to not only cover our sin, but to cleanse our blood with His very own. Having been born again through His resurrection from the dead, we carry a new genetic code, borne along throughout our entire being by His blood. The marrow of God is who we are.

Long after Abraham departed to be with the Lord, Moses came forth to deliver the people into the promises of God.

While on the mountain alone, he received the Law directly from God—a Law whose function was to lead us to Christ later on. The moral code, known as the Ten Commandments, along with the ceremonial laws, were God's way of relating to Israel, the people that He formed for His glory. Yet the Lord knew that no man could attain unto the standard of God Himself—so in love He sent Christ to empower us into union with Father, Son, and Holy Ghost.

Today there are two types of blood that flow through the hearts of two kinds of men on the earth. Those who avail of the blood of the Lord and those still living by the blood of the world. Those who are cleansed by the blood of Jesus Christ are purified through faith in Him alone. Those who refuse the blood sacrifice that He made on the cross to atone for sin are still in and of the world.

Moses enacted the first agreement between God and the people that he created for Himself, but Jesus created a whole new race of men. The Law was given by a man, but grace and truth came by the Man Jesus Christ. Through His life, death, burial, resurrection, and ascension, Jesus mediated the way for all of us to live just like Him. Alive to God, but dead to the world; buried with Him, yet seated above.

While none of the rest of God's people could approach, Moses received the Law as he communed on the mountain with the Lord. Moses besought God to "show me your glory" because he wanted to know Him personally and passionately. The Lord hid him in the cleft of a rock and caused all of His goodness to pass by—but only allowed him to see the tail end—lest the fullness overwhelm him.

As God passed by Moses, He proclaimed His Name— "The LORD, The LORD God."[78] During the course of leading His people through the wilderness, God revealed the covenant through His Name—conferring the benefits of His person upon the Israelites.

His Covenant Names are the revelation of who He is. In Christ, we take His Name as the revelation of who we are. In the former communion the Lord surnamed Himself, "The God of Abraham, Isaac, and Jacob." In this present union we rejoice in being called by the Name above all Names— Jesus. He is our Portion and we are His inheritance.

God's dealings with Moses were meant to mark the way, but never rise to the standard of all that He had planned. The glory of the risen Lord deposited forever in the heart of man is what He always had in mind. The best that we could hope to attain unto before was "never good enough" because the Law could make no man perfect. Now, through Christ we have already been raised up into His Presence—and an ever increasing dimension of the glory of God continues to fully form in and for us who believe.

The first covenant was inaugurated with incredible glory to say the least—so much so that the people of God could not even bear to look upon the Presence of the Lord in the face of Moses—the mediator between God and them. When he came down from the mountain he had to wear a veil because even the glimpse of God that he saw had the power to overpower the whole world.

Moses reflected what He beheld. The Israelites couldn't stand to steadfastly behold the face of a man, and even the man himself couldn't stand to behold the face of God. But now we are changed into His very own image and likeness from glory to glory—from one degree of being like Him to the next degree of being like Him. As we behold Him, we also reflect who He is. Moses knew Him face to face, but we know Him heart to heart. Man looks on the outward appearance and says, "It's good enough." But God looks on our innermost being and says, "There's more of Me I want you to have."

Adam was never all that God wanted to do. Abraham never saw the promises fulfilled. Moses never entered the promised land. Not the original creation, nor the age of Abraham, neither yet the glory of God in the face of Moses fulfilled the purpose and plan of Him who knows the beginning from the end.

God passed by Moses, but He passed in to us. By the blood of Jesus Christ, the goodness of God—which is His glory—is transmitted from Him into all of those who call on His Name.

This new covenant administered by Jesus is attended with such surpassing glory that the people of God not only behold Him, but are actually transfigured into His very image in ever increasing glory as we continue looking to the Mediator between God and us—the Man Christ Jesus.

Better Covenant, Better Promises

I've heard many people say in more than one way, "It's yet to be seen what God could do with the man who would give Him 100% of the glory 100% of the time." I certainly agree but say also, "In Christ we already see what God does with the man who is willing to receive 100% of the glory that God desires to confer 100% of the time."

Jesus enjoins us to "seek the praise and honor and glory which come from Him Who alone is God"[79] and says again in another place "I have given them the glory and honor which You have given Me."[80] We offend the Father through our failure to receive the richest measure of Who He is and what He makes available.

The Spirit of the Lord rested at times upon His people of old, but now because of Jesus the veil has been removed and the fullness of God dwells permanently in us. Understand though what I am not saying—you and I are not God. We will never attain unto some level of co-Godness. He is the Lord, and He is God all by Himself.

> "But you are a chosen race, a royal priesthood, a dedicated nation, [God's] own purchased, special people, that you may set forth the wonderful deeds and display the virtues and perfections of Him Who called you out of darkness into His marvelous light."
>
> —1 Peter 2:9

Just as I chose my wife to share in all that I am and all that I have, God created man to receive all that He is and all that is His. As the embodiment of Christ, we're called to put His glory on display. Like Jesus, though we inhabit the realm of flesh, blood, and earth—we walk by faith—filled with and controlled by the Spirit of God. You're the closest representation of God that people will ever see until they stand before Him face to face. When Jesus said, "I and the Father are One,"[81] that ought to be our testimony also.

"The testimony of Jesus is the spirit of prophecy."[82] Prophecy is for comfort, for consolation, for edification, and for encouragement. The entrance of His Word gives and brings light. We bear the testimony of God for the world to either admit and welcome into their hearts, or refuse and shut out of their lives.

Like Jesus we also are called to so embody the Father that we too are known as the Word made flesh and dwelling among the people of the world. Ecclesiastes 8:4 says, "Where the word of a king is, there is power." The Word of the King of kings resides in us, and when we unleash that Word it runs a powerful course in the lives of all with whom we exercise influence for God.

You may be saying, "That sounds nice, but what do I really have to give?" Because you have received as a deposit the same Holy Spirit that Jesus had on earth as a man, you also have the same Holy Spirit to spend into the lives of others as well. In Him, you have power for living and loving just like Jesus. "Whoever is joined to the Lord is one spirit with Him."[83]

You have the seven spirits of God—or as the Amplified Bible says—"the sevenfold Holy Spirit."[84] He's your Comforter, Counselor, Strengthener, Intercessor, Helper, Standby, and Advocate. He's your All in all—your everything, just as my spouse is mine and I am hers.

This is Who the Holy Ghost is in you, and this is what He does—for you, through you, and because of you—in order to honor and glorify Jesus. God will not give His glory to another in the sense of allowing anyone to take it away, but He will and He does share His glory with many others—His family.

My bride is an individual being—she is not me, and I am not her. But Elizabeth is not "another"—she is flesh of my flesh and bone of my bone—it's a great mystery, but the two of us are one. Just as "woman is [the expression of] man's glory" so also "man is the image and [reflected] glory of God."[85]

God was not created from man, but man from God. Man was not created from woman, but woman from man. The reason it was not good for man to be alone is the same reason God created us—so that He would have someone to show His love. The Lord wanted to impart Himself, so He formed man of the dust of the earth and blew into his nostrils the breath of His own life.

When God said it's not good for man to be alone, He didn't mean "lonely." There's no lack of any sort in the heart of God, and He made man in His own image, bearing His own likeness. No, when God said it's not good for man to be alone, He meant to create for him someone he could

love and serve—someone just like him to transmit his goodness unto—the very goodness of God.

God was not deficient or somehow incomplete without
man, but simply wanted to have "another" to receive,
display, and share in His glory. What brings honor to God
is the recognition of Him as the All in all. Only by saying
yes to all that He desires to give are we truly empowered to
live all for Him.

Apart from God saying yes to us in Christ, Adam must
have said the biggest yes of all time to Eve. Second only
to receiving Christ, I also said the biggest yes of my life to
Elizabeth on the day that we were joined as one before the
Lord. All of God's promises are yes and amen in Him and in
Christ Jesus, and I also am still saying yes to Him and yes
to Elizabeth.

Just as God created Eve to complement Adam, so the
Lord fashioned man in the beginning to complement Him,
and recreated us in Christ Jesus to accomplish the same
end—by receiving all that He is. The relationship that Jesus
enjoys with the Father exemplifies His plan for every one of
us also:

> "All [things that are] Mine are Yours, and all [things that are]
> Yours belong to Me; and I am glorified in (through) them.
> [They have done Me honor; in them My glory is achieved.]"
> —John 17:10

We receive unlimited love from the Lord, and that's my
chief desire of my wife as well. But I married her not really

so that I could be satisfied, but so that I could derive satisfaction in the giving of myself completely to her. I wanted someone to show my goodness to—the Lord arranged for her to receive of me and she agreed. The only reason that I'm interested in her fulfilling my desire is because I know that in me her true glory is achieved. And likewise for me—it's only in the giving of myself that she can truly receive all that God has made ready for her.

At the altar I yielded my life in favor of loving and being loved. I embraced the one who gave herself to me. In the exact way that Elizabeth received me—with her whole spirit, soul, and body—we also as the bride of Christ open our lives to all that He is. I had something to give—all of my goodness, all of my mercy, all of my loving-kindness, all of my grace, all of my everything. And she was willing to receive.

Sometimes our kids think that daddy is the boss to the exclusion of mommy. It's good that they recognize God's order and arrangement in our family life, yet still they need a more complete picture of what He has in mind for the marriage relationship. While true that God gives the final word, Jesus Christ, the first among equals, is coming again for a whole-hearted bride who shares with Him in the grace of life. Not a weak, atrophied, listless partner who has no role in how things transpire—but one perfectly united with the God of all glory in this life and forever.

Jesus came to make a way for us to return to God, but He went away to put God in us. If He hadn't returned to the glory of heaven that He had with the Father before the world began, He couldn't have sent "Another" in His place to be with us *and in us* forever.

Speaking of the Holy Ghost before He was crucified Jesus says:

> "He will honor and glorify Me, because He will take of (receive, draw upon) what is Mine and will reveal (declare, disclose, transmit) it to you.
>
> Everything that the Father has is Mine. That is what I meant when I said that He [the Spirit] will take the things that are Mine and will reveal (declare, disclose, transmit) it to you."
>
> —John 16:14-15

Jesus clearly states that the mission of the Holy Ghost is to take whatever—anything and everything—that belongs to Him and give it to us. As if that were not enough, the very next sentence from the Lord's own mouth astounds even the most receptive heart: He says everything that the Father has belongs to Him, and again repeats that the Holy Ghost is going to take all that He and the Father have—and transmit it unto the Church. Not so that we make it into heaven, but so that heaven makes it into us.

All of who we are—spirit, soul, and body belongs to the Living God. All of who He is—all of His goodness, all of His mercy, all of His loving-kindness, all of His glory belongs to us who He loved and gave Himself for.

The King James Version simply states in that same

passage that the Holy Spirit will take what belongs to Jesus and "shew" it to us. That word "shew" corresponds to the same word Moses used in saying much the same thing— "Show" me Your glory.

In Christ, the glory of God is transmitted from Him unto us. The essential nature of God Himself passes from Him into those who are willing to say yes to all that He is and all that He gives. God caused all of His goodness to pass by Moses, but He caused all of His goodness to pass in to us.

When Jesus left the earth He didn't stop being who He is—He just started being who He is in the Church. "In Him the whole fullness of Deity (the Godhead) continues to dwell in *bodily* form [giving complete expression of the divine nature]."[86] As the Body of Christ, we house the treasure of all He is. God found us hidden in the world and buried us in the living wounds of Christ. Jesus purchased us with His own blood because we are the pearl of His great love, for which He paid with the price of His own life.

The Spirit of God rested at times upon His people of old, but now the Holy Ghost dwells forever in us to honor and glorify the Name of Jesus. In order to accurately embody Christ in the earth today, we have only to stay hidden in His wounds and let the glory pass through—abiding always in the place where the water and the blood came rushing out because of love.

People go to the Holy Land to walk where Jesus did. Now Jesus walks where we do. Images of tourists along-side Orthodox Jews praying next to the Wailing Wall are common. Yet there are even more devout Israelites who actually tunnel underground below the Temple Mount. They try to get as close as possible to where the Holy of Holies would have been so that they can stick letters to the Lord in the Western Wall—thinking they can touch the heart of God. Sadly, they only know of the One who wrote the Ten Commandments with His finger on tables of stone.

By contrast Jesus lives in the core of who we are and in love has already engraved our names on the Father's heart—and His Name on ours. For that reason we cry out through the ages, "Show me Your glory. Show me Your Way. Show me Your everything."

And still today His answer is the same:

"I will give you access to all that I have, and cause you to avail of all that I AM."

Abraham was the possessor of the promises of the Most High. In Christ, the Presence of God within empowering us into ever deeper union with Him is the greatest promise that we will ever possess.

Whereas the former agreement between God and man provided only for a small strip of land, our existing covenant makes provision for us—new heavens and a new earth, wherein dwells the righteousness of God.

6

SON OF MAN, SON OF GOD

C hrist came as the Son of God to save us from our sins, and lived as the Son of Man to show us what's possible in Him—a life just like His. Not only as He was when He walked on earth, but as He is right now, seated at the right hand of God, so are we in this world.

You also are son of man, and you also are son of God. Born of a woman in the earth, and born of the Holy Ghost above. As part of the great family of God, your mission is the same as Jesus—"to seek and to save that which was lost"[87] and "to destroy the works of the devil."[88] The chief weapon given to us for gathering in to our embrace the broken, vulnerable, and poor is the same one that Jesus employed to overthrow the enemy of our souls. Love.

I've been blessed by many teachers of the Word, but only a few fathers have taught me love. Fabricius Michael is a Singaporean missionary to the Philippines—and he is such a man in the Lord. Michael spends the whole substance of his being to rescue and recover children from evil. He's my partner and friend and apostle of love to the children at the home that our ministry runs.

Every day Michael is up at 3am communing with the Lord. Not really to set an example and not to be legalistic—religious people don't even get up that early—but simply because He loves deeply. At 4am the teenagers join him for true worship and vigorous prayer as the Spirit of God directs everything. At 6am he can be found spoon feeding the infant and toddler children, loving them with God's own hands. If his pastoral responsibilities don't take him elsewhere, for the rest of the day Michael will putter around ordering and arranging the compound—making sure every detail is just right for the kids that God has entrusted into his care. Customarily, most influential pastors in the Philippines have many servants doing the same things for them that Michael does for others.

This man is a lion in the faith—one of the most respected leaders in the northern part of the country—someone that others defer to and follow. A church planter, a minister of prayer, a pastor who preaches and teaches with power. When he speaks, not only do people quiet down before God, but demons close their mouths also.

And yet unless he's standing in the pulpit, he still wears the same clothes that he wore when I first met him there 10 years ago. And he's still living in the same tiny room where he was 10 years before that. And he still takes nothing for himself in terms of salary. And everything that the Lord has placed within him doesn't get stuck, but still flows out to shape the world around with the love of God.

It's amazing that other ministers of the Gospel could envy a man with a calling like Michael, but there are those who speak poorly of his work—mostly because they're jealous for the money that flows through his hands—not understanding the will of God when it comes to lovingly serving the world. If the ones who criticize Michael had access to the same dollars they would just consume it on more luxury, instead of spending their lives on broken people. The Holy Spirit said through Paul, "I will very gladly spend and be spent for you all; though the more abundantly I love you, the less I be loved."[89]

For anyone associated with our ministry there's no question who's in charge, exercising authority at the children's home in the place of the Lord. As the head of that domain, Fabricius Michael received power from above for testifying to the love of God through the witness of his everyday life.

Needless to say, Jesus experienced difficulty also in helping others understand proper authority. The disciples constantly strived with one another concerning who would be greatest in the kingdom of God:

"Now an eager contention arose among them [as to] which of them was considered and reputed to be the greatest.

But Jesus said to them, The kings of the Gentiles are deified by them and exercise lordship [ruling as emperor-gods] over them; and those in authority over them are called benefactors and well-doers.

But this is not to be so with you; on the contrary, let him who is the greatest among you become like the youngest, and him who is the chief and leader like one who serves."

—Luke 22:24-26

Pastor Michael reminds me of this same Jesus who during His last meal before dying for us, got up from the table and girded Himself with a servant's towel—washing His disciples' feet. The King of Glory—in this age and every other—commanded us to do the same—demonstrating His Lordship through our love for one another.

Michael takes very seriously his authority to rule in the Lord by loving in His Name. One prevailing thought in scripture characterizes him perfectly, in fact it's the theme of his entire life and ministry—"Inasmuch as you did it to one of the least of these My brethren, you did it to Me."[90]

One day my friend will hear, "Come…inherit the kingdom prepared for you from the foundation of the world."[91]

We were created for rulership. But authority is not control. Real authority is power to love—and it comes only from God.

Jesus left the glory of heaven that He has always had and always enjoyed, and appeared in human form to bring that same kingdom to us. Later in life He humbled Himself still further—even to the death of the cross. In between, He characterized His own mission like this—"The Son of Man is come to seek and to save that which was lost."[92]

Though well meaning, we often misrepresent the bigger truth of what He sought to communicate by misquoting the verse. Notice what He did not say, "The Son of Man is come to seek and to save *the lost*."

Of course He came to seek and to save the lost. But the lost are only part of that which was lost. Yes, they are the biggest part, yet still only part. What was lost was the ability of the lost to not only enjoy right relationship with the Father, but to rule and reign with Him forever.

God created man to fully represent Him. Since the original intent of the relationship was derailed because of sin, the commission to accurately embody Him was broken until Jesus restored the communion of heaven and earth. The breach is this—total independence from the rule of God. The communion is this—total dependence upon the rule of God. At the cross, the interface of heaven and earth converged again in the person of Christ.

Jesus is the King of those who reign as kings, and the Lord of those who rule as lords. He has made us a nation of kings and priests unto our God, and we reign in this life and on this earth. If any man is truly in Christ, the question is—"How do you choose to rule?" Preferring one another in love or still making your boast in the world? The lord you are now determines the lord you will be—and the Lord that other people will see—if at all.

Age of the Christ

The Kingdom of God is already at hand, or "in the hand" or "a present possession"—but it's also still advancing in greater measure. The kingdom comes incrementally—"like leaven which a woman took and hid in three measures of meal till it was all leavened."[93] The disciples thought the kingdom would come all at once—that Jesus would restore the preeminence of the Jewish people and establish again the Throne of David by virtue of exercising sudden, military might.

While they were on the road to Jerusalem for the final time before His death, "they thought that the kingdom was going to be brought to light and shown forth immediately."[94] So He told them a story, and as was often His way, it seemed to have nothing to do with the questions that had arisen in their minds: (condensed paraphrase mine)

"A certain nobleman went away into a far country to obtain for himself a kingdom. And so he called his servants and entrusted to each of them the same amount of money to invest saying, "Buy and sell with these while I go and then return" or in the King James Version— "Occupy until I come."[95]

When he returned after having received the kingdom, he found that the first servant doubled his money, the second increased it by half, and the third did absolutely nothing in return for the stewardship that he had been shown. And so the first and second servants were given authority over the amount of cities that corresponded with what they had earned for the Master, five and ten respectively—while the third servant was stripped of that which he had been given to operate with.

> "And [said Jesus,] I tell you that to everyone who gets and has will more be given, but from the man who does not get and does not have, even what he has will be taken away."
>
> —Luke 11:26

In other words, "Whoever has Me and My interests at heart will be given more of Me with which to serve." Money wasn't really the point. Jesus simply used it as a tool to illustrate the heart of God. When we "occupy" until Jesus comes again—worthily representing Him and His interests, He gives us more of Him to give. Our authority to steward the heart of God increases in direct proportion to how we invest His love in the lives of others.

Yes, Jesus meant for us to understand that He was the master in the parable above. But He is also the "excellent servant" who increases the Father's investment in the world through us. He "made Himself of no reputation"[96] in order to glorify the Father through us.

Even though it doesn't make sense in light of our religious training, through His own experience as the Son of Man, Jesus revealed that the essential expression of His nature and character is that of a love slave.

> "Let this same attitude and purpose and [humble] mind be in you which was in Christ Jesus: [Let Him be your example in humility:]

Who, although being essentially one with God and in the form of God [possessing the fullness of the attributes which make God God], did not think this equality with God was a thing to be eagerly grasped or retained,

But stripped Himself [of all privileges and rightful dignity], so as to assume the guise of a servant (slave), in that He became like men and was born a human being."

—Philippians 2:5-7

Meekness defines Jesus as fully as power does. In fact, that's where power comes from—being properly submitted to the Father alone. The four Gospels record that Jesus characterized His mission in many different ways, even referring to Himself by different names—but only once did He describe His inner state of being:

"Take My yoke upon you and learn of Me, for I am gentle (meek) and humble (lowly) in heart, and you will find rest (relief and ease and refreshment and [recreation and blessed quiet) for your souls."

—Matthew 11:29

It's nearly impossible to fathom that the God of the whole universe stooped so low, condescending to us in love. According to the Word, that same gentleness makes us great.[97] Sadly, meekness is not really a very present reality in the life of the Body of Christ.

Just as in Jesus' day, the multitudes are still harassed and helpless like sheep without a shepherd. And God is still looking for someone to intercede, but most of us have not allowed room in our hearts to receive a greater deposit of His love—and therefore we have too little of Him to manifest in the actual details of our everyday lives.

Some of us are just plain cold when it comes to the heart of our Lord. How can we be born again when there's no real proof of change? No visible fruit to evidence what we have gotten of God. How can a brand new heart from above turn hard again in our chest, when the love of our Lord testifies like this:

> "I will seek that which was lost and bring back that which has strayed, and I will bandage the hurt and the crippled and will strengthen the weak and the sick, but I will destroy the fat and the strong [who have become hardhearted and perverse]; I will feed them with judgment and punishment."
>
> —Ezekiel 34:16

Once a number of years ago the Lord showed me a picture of my heart. It was encrusted with barnacles all over, and when people attempted to recline upon my breast they were ripped to shreds. Obviously, God is never like that—He is perfect rest. Jesus remained in that exact place every day—never deviating from the gentleness available to Him—and therefore the Father's heart issued forth from Him in compassion for others the way that He loved Himself.

Meekness originates from dependence upon God, and dependence is the most natural thing in the world. It's the state in which we arrived as newborn babies, and it's the state to which we must return if we want to live on proper terms with the Lord. Complete reliance upon Jesus should come easily for a born again believer, just as independence is the life breath of those not yet in relationship with the Lord. For someone who truly loves God, independence is actually much harder to walk in than surrender.

Surrender requires no effort at all.

The life of God that Jesus made possible for us ought to flow effortlessly—like drawing breath into the body. We've been breathing every second of our lives until now and never thought about it once. I'm not saying that we shouldn't be thinking about and acting on His will every moment—the mediation of our heart should wholly catch us up into the highest realms of God—but we do need to watch out lest we deviate from His path by striving in our own effort.

When the Lord woke up in the morning, He didn't wring His hands together thinking, "What do I have to do today to be the Father's Son?" or "How can I keep from going wrong?"

We're not meant to go through each day trying to get God to love us or just trying not to screw up and sin. Our destiny is to walk in a tremendous amount of victory—and destiny isn't only for the ages to come but for today. The Body of Christ needs to quit trying—trying to earn God's love by living right, trying to obey, trying to walk in love, trying to read the Bible and pray. Instead we just need to be. Be about the Father's business of believing His Word. Only then will we do the things that He has planned.

Trying and trying and trying never gets anyone anywhere. I tell struggling people all the time to just give up. The world's system of being and doing is based on the best we have to offer, and the Word of God says it's never good enough. Only in total abandonment to God's will do we experience the life that He has always designed for us—a life emptied of ourselves so that we can be filled with and controlled by the Holy Spirit. If we quit trying and just give in to being loved and loving in return, the Lord will supply everything we need to live just like Him.

The thought has never once occurred to my son—how can I get dad to love me? Yes he wants to please me so he knows to do what I ask, but he also knows my love is permanent—that his place in my heart isn't conditioned upon his right or wrong response. Of course blessing results from obedience, but love isn't based on performance. Favor is free. All I want for him is to position himself to receive by simply trusting that I will make available all that he needs.

Faith alone positions us to receive—not the need to somehow be a better person by living up to our own standards. In John 6:28 the disciples asked Jesus, "What must we do to be working the works of God?" His response catches us off guard—"Do? What do you mean do? This is the work of God—that you believe (paraphrase mine)."

Every moment of every day the Lord remained in a constant state of oneness with the Father, drinking deeply of everything He had to offer. Through our faith the Father also refreshes us moment by moment as He supplies power of the Holy Spirit for living and loving just like Jesus. We're called to demonstrate His purity, His passion, and His power in the earth today. Every expression of Him is ours to express—every moment of every day.

How could Jesus operate in such purity, passion, and power? "Because He was the Son of God" is clearly not the right answer. If He lived as the Son of God then how could He reasonably expect us to "go and do likewise" in every area of life? How could He instruct us to live according to God's standard of being, without also supplying the needed power to fulfill His plan for our design? For that matter, how could a righteous God give us any command that He does not also empower us to obey?

When Jesus spoke to the wind and waves that threatened to capsize the boat He was sleeping in, even the elements obeyed Him. The disciples marveled among themselves and asked, "What manner of man is this?" He was and is and always will be fully God. But He was and is and always will be also the same manner of man as us—born of a woman and born from above. If He acted as God when He calmed the storm with a word by saying, "Peace. Be still," then how could He upbraid them for their lack of faith, knowing that they weren't God as well?

On earth, He lived as the Son of Man entirely dependent upon His vital union with God in heaven. He continually said things like, "the Son can do nothing of Himself, but what He sees the Father do" and "I only do what I've seen the Father do, and I only speak what I've heard the Father say." The commission that we have received of Him is no different—"Just as the Father has sent Me, so I am sending you."[98]

And then He breathed on them the Holy Ghost...

For any son of man to live as the Son of God requires the same anointing of the Holy Ghost that Jesus Christ had while on the earth. He took every breath with the Father in mind and therefore exhaled the Holy Spirit throughout His everyday life.

Whatever Spirit we partake of is the same one we make available. Jesus lived on earth under the influence of one Spirit alone—the same One that He has made us to drink of—even the Spirit of Truth that proceeds from the Father.

If there's a Holy Ghost, there's an unholy one also. Satan always attempts to counterfeit and distort who the Lord is and what He does. Even those who truly desire to follow Jesus become willing partners with the work of the enemy by virtue of making "self" lord instead of Christ. The Church needs to decide who we're going to host in our lives. If the Holy Ghost is not at home upon us, then be sure that the unholy one is. Who has our attention? The spirit that entertains us is the same spirit that we entertain.

The love of God is a brutal force. The Spirit testifies through John that "For this reason the Son of God was made manifest—to destroy the works of the devil."[99] Sometimes undoing the work of the enemy is as dramatic as actually driving the very real presence of demon spirits from the body:

Once I was teaching in a Bible school when I received a call that I needed to come to the pastoral house right away. When I walked inside it was like something you would see in a horror movie. One of our students was manifesting the presence of evil to such an extent that her body was rigid, yet she trembled so violently that she was raised off of the bed where she was laying. I remember her eyes rolling back in her head and her fingers being so stiff that I couldn't even bend them. But the worst part of all was that she had such a foul and perverse look upon her face while she breathed out such abusive blasphemy against the Lord.

I immediately took authority over all the work of the enemy—binding the effect of satan, and cancelling the operation of every demon which sought to prevail in her life. The unclean spirits which one minute before had railed against us venomously went out of her with such a whimper that it startled me. She lay there limp on the bed confessing Jesus Christ as Lord, and then went straight to sleep with the look of an angel on her face.

Other times loosening the grip of the enemy involves establishing God's rule in a more quiet way that is measured over the length of many days or even months. But the roots of evil are always the same—self on the throne instead of God. That's why the devil makes his central appeal to the soul of man saying essentially, "If you will...place your mind, will, and emotions on the throne of your life to the exclusion of God, then I will..."

The people of God have authority over every work of the enemy.

We ought to be flooded with God to such an extent that no separation exists between the Word we speak and the works we do. Our lives are meant to demonstrate the very same power of Him who called us out of darkness into His marvelous light. Just as surely as purity and passion mark the man singled out for Christ, so too works of power through us display His character in us.

For the resurrection life of Jesus to flow through the whole of who we are, we need to understand that the Word of God clearly reveals that man is a three part being. We have a spirit which is our innermost personality, or heart of hearts. Our spirit is who we really are and were created to be. We have a soul which is composed of our mind or intellect, will, and emotions. And we have a body, which obviously needs no explanation. Christ came to redeem the whole man, not just to save us in part—and then to deliver the whole Kingdom unto the Father.

The power of God in heaven registers first in our innermost being. If we want to operate like Jesus, we cannot allow any delay for the heavenly transmission we receive in our heart and mind to then radiate into our actual lives. In other words, obey God in faith the first time that you hear Him speak and power will be made available, emanating out through your hands, eyes, mouth, and feet.

The spirit of Jesus communed so deeply with the Spirit of the Father that the instruction He received in His innermost being went straight down into His soul and out through His body with no effort at all on His part. Because He remained totally yielded, His soul never rose up to exercise preeminence over His spirit, and therefore His body stayed completely subject to the will of God as well.

The only reason that Jesus was the revealed will of God is because He got it from the Father. He didn't go around just making stuff up. The revelation that He received was the same revelation that He imparted. Simple as that. When He spit on the ground, made clay and anointed the eyes of a blind man, He did it because the Father told Him so in advance. We have the same opportunity to receive that Jesus had, and therefore the same divine ability to reveal what He openly displayed.

But the problem that we encounter is this—our natural inclinations cause us to filter every perception of God through the lens of the soulish realm of sense and reason. Jesus didn't have this difficulty—not because He wasn't human, but because He had no inner monologue concerning the will of God—no internal debate or discussion whatsoever happening within the deepest places of His being. His mind, will, and emotions never ruled the day because His Father in heaven taught Him explicitly what to do and what to say.

If we struggle inwardly to hear the voice of God, most likely it's because of a lack of divine order and arrangement in our lives. The Lord's rule in man looks like this—the body is subject to the soul, the soul is subject to the spirit, and the spirit subjects all to the Spirit of God. When we aren't aligned properly with the will of God, nothing works out right. In fact, everything gets worse whether we believe it or not.

Like most of us I have a friend who has tried a bunch of different diets. He's always caught up in trying to lose weight, eat right, and get in shape. He enjoys great success for a season and then gains it all back again by eating whatever he wants without exercising any discipline. One day I said to him in love:

"The reason your diets don't work is because your spirit requires of your soul and body a deep heart change." You're out of line with the will of God because your soul is in charge. Your mind isn't renewed, your will isn't fixed, and so your body's unfit."

"If you really want to live the life that God has designed, you're gonna need a lifestyle change. The deep of your spirit cries out to the deep of His for you to conjoin your will with Him. Until you answer your true heart's cry, you're gonna be miserable. You can keep trying and trying all you want, but nothing you come up with is gonna work."

The human condition without the Spirit of God is in disarray from the very start. An infant child is ruled by the bodily life—the emotions and will subjected to the desires of the fleshly appetite. If that order is messed up, the baby experiences all kinds of havoc. It's only natural—that's why God works supernaturally later in life to make us into a whole different child—His son or daughter.

To live on another plane requires being transfigured into an entirely new creation. Yet believers experience the same thing as babies—being ruled by the body, or being ruled by a soul that subjugates the spirit to its own mind and will. Very simply, our spirit desires to soar on the high places with God, but our body and soul tends to make trouble apart from proper submission to the Lord. Disorder manifests in different forms, but the bottom line is this—soul and body sickness, and a crushed and wounded spirit.

No opportunity for strife exists between spirit, soul, and body in the life of that person who is surrendered fully to the will of God. For someone totally yielded to the Lord, spirit, soul, and body on earth are not even separated by different realms but one with the Father in heaven.

Jesus restored the communion of heaven and earth. His spirit was one with the Spirit of the Father. We also are son of man and son of God—stewards of that communion. It's called the Kingdom. As we *receive* Father, Son, and Holy

Spirit into our lives, the reality of heaven transfigures the reality of everything we are. As we *release* Father, Son, and Holy Spirit from our lives, the reality of heaven transfigures the reality of the earth where we are. "Freely you have received, freely give."[100]

Out of that same posture of Oneness, Jesus went around imparting everything He had been given. Grace and peace. Love and joy. Mercy and justice. How could He do that? Because they were His to give. Later on Peter, John and everyone else who walked with the Lord gave of the Spirit in the exact same way—releasing the highest elements of the kingdom of God which they had received—and doing it all in, by, and through the Name of Jesus.

There's definite substance to God's qualities of being— love, joy, peace, etc. are substantiated by the agency of the Holy Spirit in and upon us. When the Spirit spoke through men like Peter saying, "Grace and peace be multiplied unto you through the knowledge of God and of Jesus our Lord"[101] those weren't just elaborate greetings on their part. They were imparting the substance of the Spirit of God into the lives of those with whom they exercised authority to lovingly serve.

We're called to reign as kings in this life—not only during some far off time when God has finally made every-thing just right. But now, in the midst of tribulation and distress...famine, peril, and sword, we are more than conquerors through Him who loved us.[102] Here in the heart of this present age—in the midst of the soul sickness of the world—through the reproach we endure for bearing His Name, "a vast and transcendent glory" is being produced, "never to cease."[103]

Our commission to represent Him to the people of the world has now been restored. The Christ of God atoned for our sin with His own blood, and sent us forth to rule again in His own stead—loving everyone with His own love. The Christ in us continues to bring all heaven and earth together by seeking and saving that which was lost and destroying the works of the devil.

7

DIFFUSION OF THE HOLY GHOST

When Jesus ascended, he never stopped being who He is—He just started being who He is in us. The fruit of the Spirit is *who He is*. The ministry gifts of apostle, prophet, evangelist, pastor and teacher are *who He gives*. And the spiritual gifts are *what He does*. As He was yesterday, so is He today, and so shall He be forever.

Pertaining to the fruit of the Spirit, Jesus *is* love—and all of the other facets of love—joy, peace, gentleness, goodness, etc. We personify the same character traits of Jesus as the Holy Spirit produces the fullest measure of His Presence in us. If the world is going to taste and see that the Lord is good, it will happen because they partake of His fruit in our lives.

Concerning ministry gifts, the Son of Man who walked the earth as apostle, prophet, evangelist, pastor, and teacher now lives in many men with the same respective gifting that He was and is. The Apostle sent to shape the 12 disciples has set foundational men in the Church right now; the Prophet to the woman at the well has ordained men to inspire thirsty hearts today as well; the Evangelist who heralded the kingdom of God is in season in this now instant; the Pastor who shepherded broken hearts through the wilderness and the Teacher who proclaimed Truth to the masses are all at work in the earth right now. Very simply, Jesus today is all of these gifts in those who have been given to the Church "for the perfecting of the saints, for the work of the ministry, for the edifying of the Body of Christ."[104]

And finally, the very spiritual gifts that He exercised while in the world are still in operation today in and through those who He has called. Words of wisdom and knowledge are still going forth; prophetic utterances still hit home to shape the course of hungry hearts; healings and miracles are still being performed; supernatural faith is arising like never before; tongues and interpretation of tongues still resound in the hearing of the Church and beyond.

These gifts flowed through the everyday life of Jesus—even tongues. The reason that there's no record in scripture of Jesus speaking in tongues is because heavenly language was all that He spoke. The Spirit was His native language—it just sounded like Aramaic or Hebrew to the world around Him. He spoke the language of Oneness with the Father—the words of spirit and life.

Tongues bear prophetic witness to who God is, what He's doing, and what He wants to do in the earth—the exact same things that He did in and through Jesus—and even greater works. Only the language of the Spirit can bring us into agreement with such implausible promises. As we pray in the Holy Ghost our faith increases so that we believe there will be a performance of that which God has spoken.

Everything that Jesus once was while in the world He still is today—just in us. He prophesies, He practically serves, He teaches, He exhorts. He imparts, He superintends, He does acts of love and mercy. Once the Father laid everything on the Son of Man, but today we are joint heirs together with Him. The selfsame Spirit who rested upon and remained in Jesus now divides among men the supernatural Presence of God as He wills.

And why? Why is Jesus still the product of the Spirit? Why is He still the gift of a man? Why is He still distributing supernatural power? So that the "measure of the stature of the fulness of Christ"[105] will be on display for all the earth to see and say, "Alleluia! For the Lord God Omnipotent reigns."[106]

The Church is the earthly counterpart of a heavenly reality. We are the temple of the Manifest Presence—the Presence manifested. And yet, "behold, there is One greater than the temple."[107] God's glory is not dependent upon us, but neither is it exclusive of us. Having been assembled together as the habitation of God, our mission is the same as the Holy Ghost—to glorify Jesus by making Him known.

God's chosen way to accomplish this was to make us One. Only as we fully embody Him will the world know and believe that the Father sent the Son. Love is the perfect and complete embodiment of God. God is love, and as we dwell in love, we dwell in God, and God in us.

"In Him the whole fullness of God continues to dwell in *bodily* form, giving complete expression of the divine nature."[108] We show forth the beauty of Jesus because we're the home of His infinite majesty. Every one of us called by His Name has received the Gift of Him—and so we're called to minister the same, "as good stewards of the manifold grace of God."[109]

Throughout the history of His dealings with the humanity He created, in Spirit, God has always been personally present. Even after Jesus left the earth, Christ still remained with us in the person of the Holy Ghost. Not many days later, in fulfillment of the promise of the Father, the followers of Jesus became "little Christs" as they were diffused throughout their whole being with the Spirit of God. He who they had known to always be with them was now in them according to the Word the Lord had spoken.

After He was crucified and raised up, Jesus ascended to where He was before so that He could become the answer to His own prayer by making us One with Father, Son, and Holy Ghost. If He had never gone away even after He arose, the disciples would have eventually gone back to not believing that He was everything that He told them.

As the Son of Man He had to leave because they couldn't see God fully in the Man until God came fully to be in them. They couldn't see that He was God even though they could see that He was the Son of God. "Beloved, now we are the sons of God, and it does not yet appear what we shall be: but we know that, when He shall appear, we shall be like Him; for we shall see Him as He is."[110] Jesus had to die, rise again, and go back to heaven before they could really believe that they too could become One with Him.

Once we fully believe, we fully receive. Jesus sends the Holy Ghost who proceeds from the Father to empower us into union with Him on the deepest possible level—always giving us an ever increasing measure of His Divine Nature.

In like manner I steward and jealously guard the heart of my wife Elizabeth. Whoever touches her touches me—whether to bless or to harm. Though she's a separate and distinct personality—she is not me and I am not her—her very nature is borne into my being, and mine into hers. We're one in spirit, one in soul, and one in body—joint heirs together of the grace of life. If I give of myself, I give in like measure of her.

I will never attain unto some level of being Elizabeth, and neither will she ever attain unto some level of being me. She will always be Elizabeth, and I will always be Tommy. But for all other intents and purposes, she is me as I am her. It's a great mystery, but I speak concerning Christ and the Church. Jesus spent the entire substance of His being for us, and men ought always to so love their wives.

Through our knowledge of God the fabric of His being is woven into ours, and new life emerges. Knowledge of

God speaks not of a set of accumulated facts in some filing system of the mind stored up for quick reference at the appropriate time. Instead, true knowledge refers to the deep, intimate, heartfelt sharing in another Life. Adam had knowledge of his wife Eve and she bore a son. "For this reason shall a man leave his mother and father, and shall cleave unto his wife, and the two shall become one."[111]

As we "cleave to the Lord with purpose of heart,"[112] fruit is borne that is consistent with the level of relationship we enjoy. The Word of God clearly states that His Divine Seed remains within us[113]—the very Life-force that controls and directs who we become. The Spirit of God speaking through Paul says, "Whoever is joined to the Lord is one spirit with God."[114]

Although we're truly one in every dimension of our lives—spirit, soul, and body—and love God with all of our heart, all of our mind, and all of our strength, there are still different levels of our experience in relationship with Him. For example, anyone can be used by God—He even spoke through a donkey once. But we are servants.

Yet even though we have yielded control and enjoy being implements of righteousness, we're not just tools in His hands. Yes we desire to serve Him with all that we are, but we've grown deeper in love and surpassed a mere servant's role because He calls us friends.

But although we're friends to the extent that we have a part in what He's doing as co-laborers together with Him, we have entered in to something far beyond mere friend-ship because the Word says that even now we are the sons of God—joint heirs together with Christ.

The Word further says that all of those who are led by the Spirit of God are the sons of God, but still there's some-thing better than being a son of God—being one with God. In fact, the only thing better than being a son is being One.

So also the only thing better than being a parent is being a husband or wife. Elizabeth has a lot of different roles. God uses her to get things done in our family life. She works for us like an instrument in the hand of the Lord, but obvi-ously she's so much more. She's also a servant motivated by love—in the church, at home, and many times even for those she doesn't know. She's also a close friend to many—someone who shares in the joy and pain of life alongside those with whom she enjoys relationship. She's also the daughter of her mother and father, and a wonderful mother to our son and daughters.

But above all else, she's one with me—one who shares completely in all that she is and likewise receives of all that I am. There's no higher calling for Elizabeth Green, and neither is there any higher role for me.

If she wants to be used by God, our oneness must be intact. If she wants to serve the church and those outside as well, our oneness must be intact. If she wants to extend the deepest level of friendship possible to those who the Lord brings into her life, our oneness must be intact. If she wants to honor her mother and father, if she wants to be a good mother to our son and daughters, then our oneness must be intact. If she wants to "hold the thoughts, feelings, and purposes"[115] of my heart, then our oneness in spirit, soul, and body must be intact.

And I must love her as I love my very own life. It's the best thing I can do to honor Christ, the best thing I can do to be a good father, and the best thing I can do to be an able minister of the Gospel—fitted and qualified by God with the anointing of His own person.

Jesus endured the suffering and the shame on our behalf—esteeming it as nothing—compared with the joy set before Him of gathering us into His embrace. Not just as His bride—but as His very own flesh—the Body of Christ—delighting in us as His very own life.

Truly what we have to give is the composition of God Himself. The reception of the highest elements of the kingdom of God is due to His Presence operating in and upon our lives. In and through our knowledge of God, the substance of the Spirit is multiplied.

The problem with our conception of God is that we have thought of Him as being immaterial—and therefore have constituted Him thus—as though it were up to us to make of Him what we will. God is not an immaterial being. God is Spirit, and Spirit is the most concrete substance in the universe and beyond. In all of heaven and earth, no matter what dimension, there's nothing more tangible than the Presence of God.

Diffusion of the Holy Ghost

As citizens of another realm, our mission is the same as Jesus—to impart the substance of the world in which we're from into the world in which dwell. When Jesus spoke to the wind and waves, the elements of earth obeyed because the heart of God came forth to overpower every other force. The peace of the kingdom where Jesus reigned flowed out from His innermost being to change the kingdom of this world into the kingdom of our Lord. What was in Him came out of Him to define the world around Him.

The Spirit of God is the most definitive reality in the universe. Clearly there's no force equal to or greater than the Holy Ghost. When we release the highest elements of the kingdom of which we're from, the love of God transfigures the entire course of human nature in the hearts of those willing to receive the miracle wherever we are.

Freely we have received, freely we give. There's nothing greater than to be born again from above, but we didn't stop there when it came to receiving all that God makes available, and so we don't stop there when it comes to releasing all that He desires to impart as well. "He who spared not His only Son but delivered Him up for us all, how shall He not through Him freely give us all other things also?"[116]

Jesus spoke of imparting our peace into whatever situation we encounter. He instructed us to give our blessing to any house that we enter by first saying, "Peace be to this house."[117] He said that if a man of peace dwelt there, then our peace would remain; but if not, then our peace would return unto us from where it came.

Age of the Christ

Like spirit attracts like spirit. Like Jesus and like Paul, we long to impart the Spirit as well—through the laying on of hands, and through the Word of Life that we hold forth. The Gift of God is who we have received, and so the Gift of God is who we give. We're called to demonstrate the Holy Ghost. Not to display our gifts, but to display our God. For too long the Church has sought to be known for the operation of our gifts, instead of the operation of our God.

Christ in us is a vital fragrance for those around us who are being saved as well. Contrariwise, when the desire for God is absent from a person's life, it's very difficult to impart grace and peace because there's no room in them to receive. In Christ, the Father has re-constituted us so that infinite capacity exists to receive the wealth of Jesus in the Holy Ghost. We therefore possess infinite capacity to bless others with Him who is our Portion and Inheritance.

We're called to operate as brokers of the wealth of Jesus. Grace is wealth in and of the Holy Ghost which God makes available to us and then distributes through us. Wealth is what heaven has. No one subject to that realm is believing for true riches because we've already received Him. But the people all around us have not yet availed of the Gift of God—His grace. The elements of the kingdom are a heavenly reality existing in us that have no earthly counterpart except we release them into the lives of those who we serve.

Grace and peace are of the highest order in the kingdom of God in heaven and earth. Just as salvation encompasses so much more than being saved from our sin and on our way to heaven, so also the means of salvation—grace—encompasses so much more than simply "unmerited favor."

Grace is not only the wealth of God given to us, but it's power of the Holy Ghost for living and loving just like Jesus. However He lived when He walked the earth, and however He lives right now seated at the right hand of God, we also are so empowered.

"Whoever says he abides in Him ought [as a personal debt] to walk and conduct himself in the same way in which He walked and conducted Himself."

—1 John 2:6

How He lives right now is how He lived then—full of purity, passion, and power. We're called to the exact same life because "as He is, so are we in this world."[118] Not only as He was, but as He is, and will forever be—so also are we. The life of God is impossible with men; but to those who believe what the Lord said, faith closes the distance between where we are and where Jesus intends for us to live.

Like grace, peace is so much more than what we think. Yes, it speaks of soul harmony and concord with God, of freedom from discord within and without. But the shalom of God is so much more—it's the very God of Shalom. Peace is not just the absence of some thing, but the Presence of some One.

Peace is the perfect well being of God Himself. Jesus took the pains of our punishment that were necessary to obtain our peace. If we have the perfect well being of the Lord what more could we need? Peace is everything necessary for our own good and His own glory—and every spiritual blessing in abundance in the heavenly realm even while we live right here. Our Father has promised to supply all our need according to His riches in glory in Christ Jesus, and all He wants us to do is just receive.

Make no mistake. The will of God if for us to experience grace and peace in every area of our lives—spirit, soul, and body. Just because they don't happen to exist in the fullest measure in our present circumstances does not negate His desire to say "yes and amen"[119] to all that He has promised. The Lord's heart is for the kingdom to be ours in ever increasing measure—for grace and peace to be multiplied to us abundantly in and through the knowledge of God.

No word that God has spoken is ever without power of fulfillment—not one Word will ever fail. God spoke to Moses to build the tabernacle according to the instruction that he received on the mount, so that He would dwell among His people Israel. God promised Noah that if he built the ark, a type of Christ, to the exact dimensions uttered from God's own mouth, that he would be saved while the whole world drowned. Solomon prepared the temple according to the design of the heavenly manifest with one promise in mind—that God would be manifest there.

In Christ, the lower parts of the earth—human nature apart from God—have been infused with the Life of Jesus.

As the Lord continues to minister unto us out of His own substance—we continue being filled with the Holy Ghost. We're One with Him who has appeared on earth to take away sin, and who appears in heaven as the minister of the sanctuary, and the true tabernacle, which the Lord pitched, and not man.

Just because we're in the world doesn't mean that we serve only under the shadow of heavenly things to come. Even right now we're ministers of the Spirit unto men and unto God from our vantage point of being positioned with Christ in heavenly places. It's from here that we look for the appearing of our Lord, and it's from here that we display the wonders of Him who we behold.

God the Son did what no other man ever could. We have such a High Priest, who is set on the right hand of the throne of Majesty in the heavens—and we're seated with Him there as priests unto our God, even as we reign on the earth in this now season.

We have no might, no power, and no ability of our own. Our sufficiency is of God. As able ministers of the Spirit, Christ has made us dispensers of the new covenant established on the best that God has to offer. Our ministry is to make known the standard of heaven which Jesus clearly stated, "Your kingdom come, Your will be done; as in heaven, so in earth."[120]

When I started out in ministry the Lord sent me to a place called the Galilean Children's Home. I lived there for one year so that Jesus could teach me how to love. Jerry Tucker and his wife Sandy founded the work to rescue and recover children from the snare of the enemy. They have literally become "Dad and Mom" to hundreds of kids from all over the world.

Sandy passed away in 2007. Since then Jerry has mentioned in every newsletter, almost without exception, Sandy's heart and desire for the ministry to go forth so that more kids will be touched for the glory of God. This is not only a man who longs for his companion of almost 50 years. This is Jerry Tucker, the steward of a heavenly reality that has no earthly counterpart except he release it—namely, the heart of Sandy—the very heart of God.

We're called to impart and release the substance of God's own heart—grace and peace—from the heavenly realm that we call home into the earthly realm that we occupy until He comes.

Whatever happens in heaven, where the rule of God reigns because His will is done—can, should, and will happen right here on earth.

8

THE CHIEF SINGER

The Church needs to attune our hearing to the sound of heaven. As we listen for God and respond accordingly, we position ourselves to receive the richest measure of who He is and what He makes available. The conversation becomes such beautiful communion that eventually it turns into a song—catching us up into the Presence of the Divine.

In the beginning Father, Son, and Holy Spirit communed saying, "Let Us make man in Our image, according to Our likeness."[121] Yet even before then, God in His foreknowledge had each one of us in mind—and in that sense we existed in Him before the age of time. When the days were accomplished for us to be delivered into flesh and blood, we emerged from the bosom of God—and then broke forth from the womb according to the fullness of His design.

Today, very simply, because of our sin, God intervened in Christ to repair the breach between us and Him. Through

Jesus we've escaped the corruption of this present world, having been born again from above in a sovereign and supernatural act of God. According to His own purpose and grace which was given to us before the world began, we've been gathered once again into His embrace so that we—us and Him—enjoy the pleasure of consummating all that He has planned.

The Breath of God that gave us life in the very beginning is the same gentle whisper of the Spirit that continues today and will forever resonate throughout our whole being. When we hear the voice of the Lord full of such majesty, in us—the temple of the Holy Ghost—every atom of who we are cries out for the glory of God.

The Lord gave me the names of my two oldest children, but He personally named my youngest child. When my wife was halfway through her pregnancy, the Spirit woke me in the middle of the night with these simple words, "Her name is Bethel."

Elizabeth and I had been wondering what to call her—we knew that she was a girl, but hadn't come up with a name. It was definitely God who awakened me that day, but I sort of very casually had this thought anyway, "OK Lord, yeah whatever, I'm going back to sleep."

Not too spiritual huh? Reminds me of a lot of other people in scripture when God showed up to do something beautiful.

Later on when I got up that morning to pray I had already forgotten how the Lord had spoken so dramatically just a few hours earlier. As I quietly waited upon Him, once again the Voice of the Lord resounded in my hearing—"Her name is Bethel."

This time, without any thought whatsoever, I said, "Yes Lord, absolutely, her name is Bethel."

Elizabeth and the other two kids were still sleeping that day when I went off to the hotel where I worked answering phones at the front desk. I called home at the time that she normally awakened to tell her the news—"Her name is Bethel."

Even though I excitedly recounted what the Lord had done and said, she didn't like hearing it at all. That's less a reflection on her heart and more of just a mother's initial response to a prospective baby name that she really doesn't like. But I knew that the Word of the Lord would stand, so I patiently said, "Just wait, you'll see."

That same morning, no more than two hours later, God confirmed the word He had spoken with a prophetic sign that filled me with incredible wonder. About 11am I answered a call for an employee at the hotel who wasn't available. When I asked to take a message the lady replied, "Just tell him that Bethel called."

I almost fell out of my seat. "Can you repeat your name please?'

"Bethel."

"B-E-T-H-E-L?"

"Yeah, just tell him I called please."

I hung up the phone and immediately dialed my own number, "Honey you're never going to believe this—a woman named Bethel just called the hotel."

She probably wanted to smack me, but knew that I wasn't just fooling around. Neither one of us had ever even heard of a person named Bethel—we only knew the word to be a proper noun referring to a place name. I had ministered extensively in two congregations named Bethel—in Hawaii and overseas—and had actually asked Elizabeth to marry me inside the sanctuary at Bethel Community Church in the Philippines. But I'm not even sure that I really ever knew what it meant—house of God.

Elizabeth said, "I still don't care, we're not naming her Bethel." Okay, at this point in the narrative it's getting a little more difficult for me to defend her apparent hardness of heart to the move of God. Still though, a pregnant mother is naturally quite possessive of her child—so I knew that I just needed to allow her room to grow into His will for our life.

"Just wait, you'll see," I told her again.

For about two months I didn't mention another word, and we didn't talk about any other names either. Until one day she came to me out of the blue and said, "Yeah, her name is Bethel."

That may seem like just a cute story, but when God Himself names your baby, that's something special. Obviously He doesn't do anything for no reason—especially something as important as what a child will be called. Maybe only He knows why at this point, but in naming Bethel personally that puts her in some pretty interesting company—Isaac, Solomon, John, and JESUS.

Maybe that sounds like a daddy just wanting to be proud of his child, but maybe God wants to name all of our babies and we just don't know it because we don't really listen the way we should. That He wants to name all of our children is probably an exaggeration, but the principle remains the same—God is still speaking today, and we need to sensitize ourselves to hear what He's saying.

When my family lived in a smaller house it was always very difficult for me to find a place to pray without being disturbed or disturbing anyone else. Early in the morning while everyone still slept I would often get down on the floor by the bed. I used to keep a little lamp out in the corner with the Word open before it, and there I would seek the Lord before every day started.

Many times when I was lifting up my children to God, Bethel would sneak into the room, climb quietly up on the bed while her mother slept, and hang over the edge where I would be praying below. Because she was very still, sometimes I knew she was there, and other times not.

Without saying a word, Bethel more than once heard me praying over her something like this:

"Father I thank you for the great future that You have prepared for Bethel Aquino Green. I thank you that it was you

who took her from the womb and caused her to hope when she was upon her mother's breast.

"I thank You that according to Your word, Bethel and her sister Micah are cornerstones, polished after the similitude of a palace. Cornerstones of great families—mothers who will bring forth thousands and ten thousands even though now they're just young girls. I thank you that they're blessed with blessings of the heavens above and of the earth below. Blessed with blessings of the breasts and of the womb."

Even though I was often unaware that Bethel was in my presence, the Father always knows exactly where we've come from, where we are, and where we're going. When we quiet down our lives to hear from God, we enter in to a conversation already taking place concerning us in the heavenly realm.

Thankfully as children of the Most High we have the freedom, courage, and boldness to charge in to the Presence of God the same way that our children come fearlessly into ours. Yet oftentimes the busyness of our own minds and consequently the busyness of our own lives prevents us from hearing the deep of His Spirit calling to the deep of ours.

Bethel is my daughter by birth, but she may never know the fullness of who I am and what I make available as her father unless she quiets down her life to experience me on the deepest possible level. When the thoughts of her own mind take precedence over my desires for her life, then her entire destiny is in danger of being lost.

Just like our Heavenly Father—in my wisdom, power, and goodness I have prepared a path ahead of time for my children to walk upon. If they will just place their little hands in mine instead of carving their own way through life, then I'll certainly lead them along in manner that is only good for them.

For everyone who is called by His Name our future is exactly the same—to be changed in and by the Presence of God to become increasingly more like Jesus until that day when we see Him face to face. As we behold Him we are constantly being transfigured into His own image from glory to glory—from one degree of being like Him to the next degree of being like Him.[122]

We behold Him in the Word. We behold Him in the inner witness of our hearts bearing witness with the Holy Spirit that we are the sons of God. We behold Him in all manner of prayer. We behold Him in fellowship with one another. We behold Him in worship. We behold Him in silence. We behold Him in service to others. We behold Him in creation. When we earnestly seek Him, we behold Him everywhere.

But there's an entire generation on the earth today who have never seen God at all—in large part because they've grown up without an earthly father who walks with the Lord. It's an epidemic throughout the world—the parent that the Heavenly Father appointed to make Himself known has abdicated his role and left only a void instead. Consequently this generation is unlike any other who have come before in the sense that their identity has been derived from a source other than what God ideally desires. Partly because of fatherlessness in the natural realm, there are more lost people now than ever.

No matter who we are though, none of us are going to be like the Father unless we spend time with the Father. One of the chief roles of any dad is to raise up his child into a place of inward and outward sufficiency, and that requires discipline. Clearly God corrects us so that we finally come to and forever abide in a place of having renounced all claims to self—so that we see that our sufficiency is of Him. When we grow up into Christ in all things, we enjoy release from God into the life to which we're called.

Chastening is painful, but it produces a resolve to rely upon the Father that we would not have otherwise had. Even the Lord Jesus had no chance of growing into the Son He was called to become without learning obedience through the things He suffered.[123] Throughout all the days of His flesh, Jesus modeled death as the only real path to life. Only as we identify with His power of putting to death the innumerable aspects of self, do we also partake of His resurrection life.

When Jesus took Peter, James, and John up into a high mountain to pray, as He began to seek the Father, suddenly His whole countenance changed. He appeared no longer as they had always known Him, but how He was to become once He returned to the majesty from where He came. As Peter and the others got a foretaste of the Risen Christ of

God, they trembled at the express image of the Father in the person of the Lord.

Moses and Elijah appeared with Jesus there in glory also and "spake of His decease which He should accomplish at Jerusalem."[124] The Lord's whole mission on earth was to give His life as a ransom for many—Jerusalem spoke of the culmination of His entire reason for being. That's why He constantly stated, "Behold, we go up to Jerusalem, and all things that are written by the prophets concerning the Son of man shall be accomplished."[125]

There was a conversation taking place in the heavenly realm that the Lord needed to enter in to hear. The words spoken over Him by Moses and Elijah furthered His desire to depart from this life—so that the Law and the Prophets could be fulfilled—through the death and resurrection of the Messiah who He was and is.

Prior to ascending the mountain Jesus had said, "There are some standing here who shall not taste death till they see the kingdom of God"[126] come in power. If we would only die as the normal course of everyday life, then death wouldn't run its course. But God won't crucify us for us—we have to do it ourselves. Just like Isaac who prefigured Jesus many centuries before, we have to become a living sacrifice also—willing to offer ourselves on the cross as the highest expression of worship to God.

The cross that Jesus bore in death was the same one that He carried in life—it was just made manifest for all to behold at Calvary. His external reality reflected His inner state of being of "not My will, but Yours be done." Only a dead man allows Himself on the cross—because only a man who is already dead knows he can truly live again.

Remember, they spoke of that which He had to fulfill—His death, or exodus from this life. Death is the greatest achievement that any of us will ever accomplish. Death to our own hopes, dreams, ambitions, and desires apart from the will of God. Death to everything outside of His rule and reign in our lives. Death to our own way of being and doing once and for all time—so that He who "is able to [carry out His purpose and] do superabundantly, far over and above all that we [dare] ask or think [infinitely beyond our highest prayers, desires, thoughts, hopes, or dreams]" will be glorified in Christ Jesus and the church forever and ever."[127]

The Lord's constant and unsettling injunction when He walked the earth was always "Why wait? Die now, so that you can truly live," but no one else really seemed to get it. For example, when Jesus was transfigured and in every other instance prior to His resurrection, Peter didn't want anything to do with dying. On the mountain he was an eyewitness to the majesty and obviously wanted to encamp in the beauty of what he beheld there forever. Peter didn't understand then that the way to eternal glory comes only through the cross of Christ. Not knowing what to say, he blurted out:

"Master, it's good for us to be here. And let us make three tabernacles: one for You, one for Moses, and one for Elijah."[128]

While he was still speaking the Heavenly Father began to overshadow them in a cloud, and immediately they were "sore afraid." Then the voice of God came forth from above saying, "This is My Son, My Beloved, with Whom I am [and have always been] delighted. Listen to Him!"[129]

And then just as suddenly as the glory that Peter had hoped would last forever happened, everything disappeared. The exceeding grandeur of the vision was gone, and they were left alone to descend the mountain with the same Jesus they had always known. But Peter, James, and John were changed forever because they heard the words spoken in the heavenly realm even while they were still standing here.

Not only was Peter an eyewitness to the majesty[130], but he actually heard the voice of God from above charging him to listen. Still he didn't understand—to remain in the glory of God forever, we can't rush in prematurely—without first having shared a death like Jesus.

Destiny unfolded for everyone on the mountain in that particular moment. Moses and Elijah experienced the initial fulfillment of Him Who they had foreshadowed. The Lord Jesus was more encouraged than ever to continue on the path of the Father's choosing. And Peter, James, and John trembled like little children at the sound of the Voice of God borne out of heaven.

Unless we all humble ourselves under the mighty hand of the Lord and become like mere children, we will in no way experience the kingdom. If we are to inherit *Him* and all that has been prepared for us from the foundation of the world, we can only enter in as a little child.

When my kids were infants they all delighted to hear the wonders of my voice and behold my facial expressions of love. As I played with them, laughing and making silly faces, they would be so caught up in me that nothing else mattered.

As small children they were never influenced by the things of this life—neither things before nor things behind. They were marvelously free from not only opinions concerning themselves or any other, but free from thoughts of the past or the future. Totally without care.

Look into the eyes of any baby, and he is just *there*—rapt in your own eyes—not consumed by anything else in that moment of time. A baby continually abides in the exactness of the now—not in the future, not in the past. We also are called to live out our destiny in Christ every second—not in some far off time and not in days gone by—but moment by moment with Him who was and is and is to come—yesterday, today, and forevermore.

Yet not only is there a conversation concerning us occurring in the heavenly realm where we're positioned with the Father in Christ Jesus, but there's also a song of the Spirit that He wants us to hear so that our destiny will be fulfilled.

Right now if we can learn to be quiet enough to listen for the voice of God singing over us, then we'll certainly hear His heart for the Beloved who we are in Christ.

David was a man "after God's own heart"[131] who was destined to be a king. A man in pursuit of God, but also a man "according to God's own heart" or, "with a heart like God." The Lord took Him from following after sheep where he had learned to abide in the secret place of the Most High—down at His feet, overshadowed by His Presence. He desired one thing above all else—to dwell in that same place moment by moment everyday—in the Presence of the Lord.

David eventually had everything that the world could offer, yet his highest delight was beholding the face of God. David knew the joy of being in the Lord's heart, and the joy of the Lord being in his. The sweet psalmist of Israel sang because he heard His Father singing first. He danced because he saw His Father dance. He was wrapped in the embrace of God so intimately that in a very real sense the worshiper and the Worshipped became One.

David knew this truth—that the joy of the Lord is our strength. Not only the joy the Father imparts, but the joy that is His very own—the kind that only a father can know. The pleasure exclusive to heaven alone is borne on the facial expression of our Father God as He celebrates us with unfailing love.

If we would meditate on the expression of pure delight on the face of God as He looks upon our lives, we would then hear and know that the same testimony He had for His only begotten Son, He also has for us—"this is My Beloved in whom I am well pleased." If we only beheld His joy, we would be impelled by the very Spirit within us into the highest possible dimension of being in Him.

My son Jed knows my joy and my displeasure. If love is the basis, then both should motivate him to grow into the fullest stature of the man he's called to become. Yet even though I discipline Him in love, there's something about my joy in particular that spurs him on. Likewise for us, knowing the pleasure of God moves us to continue pushing further and further into the high places that only He foreknows for our lives.

Jed's only 9 right now and most of the time he acts pretty goofy around the house. If he can see that his behavior brings delight to me—that I'm getting a kick out of him—then he keeps going on and on. But obviously, at times there's no place for his antics, and if I shoot him a cross look, he slumps his shoulders, hangs his head, and shuffles off dejected. It's amazing what the facial expression of a father can accomplish at the appropriate time.

The Lord guides us with eyes so full of adoration that we ought to be overwhelmed with desire to become all that He has planned. His joy is for us to be wrapped in His arms of love, and that's why He enjoins us to "seek the praise and honor and glory which come from Him Who alone is God."[132]

Jed requires my praise as a vital necessity in his life. As children of God, the joy of the Lord—that joy which is exclusively His own—empowers us, provokes us, and spurs us on to continue pressing toward the mark of our highest calling in Him.

But without intimacy, we won't hear the call. Without intimacy, God has no opportunity to sow the seed of His Presence into the deep of our spirit. If the seed of God isn't sown, if it doesn't root down deep, grow up strong, blossom and bear fruit—then how is the world going to be filled with the knowledge of the glory of Him?

There's a war taking place in the heavenlies to prevent the Godly seed that the Lord has always sought to propagate from taking root in the earth today.

The reason that "the sons of God beheld the daughters of men, that they were fair"[133], is because *The* Son of God had already done that. From time immemorial, the Lamb slain from the foundation of the world had already made a way for us to return to God. The enemy always tries to counterfeit and corrupt the seed of the One who has fixed the beauty of His gaze upon the children of men.

By the grace of His atoning sacrifice and our reception of the divine nature through faith, Jesus Christ formed an entirely new race unto God who populate heaven and earth today. We're a new creation of the Lord, and He's the Father of this whole family—the Church.

Satan has been referred to popularly at times as the "chief worship leader in heaven" before he was cast down for trying to lift his own glory above the throne of God. He may have been a worship leader once, but He never could have been a true worship giver. No one can worship God and exalt himself at the same time.

The strategy of the adversary has always been to motivate men to seek their own glory—just like him. In Genesis 11 when he inspired the human race to make a name for themselves in heaven, God Himself dismantled the Tower of Babel, and confused their language to keep them from accomplishing a counterfeit destiny. "Nothing they imagine will be impossible with them."[134]

But the devices of the enemy and the plans of men apart from God always come crashing down. He confused their language during that day, but later on infused ours with the life of heaven itself. If we all speak with the tongue of the One who has already spoken, nothing will be impossible because not one Word from God is ever without power of fulfillment.

The Word of the Lord is settled forever in heaven—we need to let it sink down, hit home, and find bottom in the deep of our being. Listen to the Spirit from cover to cover throughout scripture and hear the beautiful Voice of Majesty singing endearingly over all His creation:

Listen to the final Word of God in Revelation 22:17 as the Spirit and the Bride together say, "Come." Listen to the Song of Moses and the Song of the Lamb in Revelation 15, whose voices in unison glorify the Sovereign of Ages and King of the Nations. Listen to Paul who was caught up into the third heaven and heard utterances that were too wonderful to recount. Listen to the Acts of the Apostles, and see what happened when the Spirit moved the Church to function in one accord. In the atmosphere created through ministering to the Lord and fasting, the Holy Spirit spoke and the lives of those who heard were changed forevermore.

Listen to Isaiah—he became an instrument so attuned to the voice of God that he was actually positioned to hear Father, Son, and Holy Ghost saying to One another, "Whom shall I send, and who will go for Us?" Then he whose lips had just been cleansed by what happened in the heavenly realm, entered in to the conversation himself—answering the call of God by saying, "Here am I, send me."[135]

How could Isaiah go to a people whose ears were dull of hearing with a message like "keep on listening" without first having his own lips cleansed and his own sin forgiven? The only reason that he was ready to speak is because he had already listened.

Listen again to the Spirit who speaks in Jeremiah 33 of a day when the voice of the Bridegroom and the Bride will sing together in sacred communion.

Listen to God who compassed David about with songs of victory and caused him to hear His own song which became David's prayer to the God of his life—the same One who gave Job songs in the night.

Listen to Enoch who walked with God and was not, for the Lord took him. He was caught away because their fellowship became too sweet for him not to be translated to a higher dimension of being. Their walk grew so inter-twined that one day instead of Enoch going back home afterward, the Lord just brought him to His own. He knew the majesty of the Maker of the Universe singing over his life, and surrendered in love to the sacred voice of the One who has heaven for His throne—the One who even the heaven of heavens cannot contain.

And how about us? The Word of God says that the High and Exalted One who inhabits eternity dwells there also with us. How astounding! Just think of it. We were right there in the Lord's embrace, singing together when He laid the Cornerstone of the whole earth. As sons of God by faith in Christ Jesus we were gathered with Him in the begin-ning, sounding out praise "when the morning stars sang together and all the sons of God shouted for joy"[136]—right there present in Christ, the Lamb slain from the foundation of the world.

The point is this—there's a prophetic utterance taking place in the heavenlies beyond the power of anyone on earth but the Holy Ghost to express. Through the Spirit of God, we have an Anointing that abides permanently within—an unction from the Holy One, and we know all the things of His Spirit if we will only position ourselves to listen.

The song of the Spirit is like hearing the voice of your mother from the womb. Elizabeth sang to our children from the time of conception until birth—they always knew and recognized her voice. The Lord sang a sacred lullaby over our lives from the very "womb of the morning"[137]—before time existed.

> "The Lord hath called me from the womb; from the bowels of my mother hath He made mention of my name."
>
> —Isaiah 49:1 KJV

Since the foundation of the world until even now in the night seasons of our earthly lives, His song enraptures us—perfecting praise out of the mouth of babes through songs that we recall from a long ago realm of being in Him.

I remember going in at night and singing over my children as they slept—songs which somehow made a way into their consciousness. I never really had to sing them to sleep, but I would often go in to check and see how they were doing and sometimes just stand there in awe for what seemed like hours. Especially when they were really little, I was the most amazed father on earth—as I watched them resting sweetly my heart was always overcome with delight.

The Spirit of God speaks through Zephaniah of quieting us with His love.[138] Imagine God, the Creator of Heaven & Earth rejoicing over His children with joy and exulting over us with singing. Incredible. What a wonder—the Lord Himself twirling about our lives in a dance of delight that catches us up into His embrace.

The Hebrew word picture used in Zephaniah is very similar to the same one employed by the Spirit through

Habakkuk[139]—only in this instance it's us rejoicing in the Lord, the God of our salvation. In the language of the Holy Ghost, exult means to "rejoice greatly" and rejoice means "to twirl with great intensity."

Just like a mother and child, a father and son, or a husband and wife—imagine us delighting in Him until the worshiper and the Worshipped finally become One.

All of these pictures of family life are really the best snapshots we have of the Godhead and His love for not only us, but Himself. On every level Father, Son, and Holy Spirit enjoy the deepest possible agreement—reverencing One another greatly and sharing incredible honor among themselves. Jesus extols the Father, the Holy Ghost glorifies Jesus, and the Father praises the Son.

We too are filled with God—Father, Son, and Holy Ghost dwell permanently within us. His voice broke through our sin hardened hearts until we were born again from above in the exact moment that He predestined in love for us to be conformed to the image of His Son.

Jesus says, "The time is coming, and now is, when the dead shall hear the voice of the Son of God: and those who hear shall live."[140] The Holy Spirit opened our ears, and now that we experience the fullness of the Lord through agreement with His will, just like Jesus on earth, we also are a habitation of the Living God.

Other than when He sang hymns on the night of His betrayal, no historical record exists in either of the four

Gospels of Jesus ever singing. But the truth is that He was, is, and always will be the Chief Singer.[141] There is no other beside the Son who can or ever will extol the Father so extravagantly on this side of heaven—and yet He's reproducing the same glory in us who are called by His Name.

As we quiet our self life to hear the conversation taking place concerning us in the heart of God, like Jesus, the melody of heaven will rain down without measure upon our earthly lives.

9

THE TESTIMONY OF JESUS

Revival comes when the fire of God shut up in our bones finds another place to burn. Revival inevitably changes not only the composition of the earth we are and the earth upon which we walk, but even the face of heaven itself eventually becomes more crowded with once lost souls.

When I was a small boy I liked to play with fire. My grandmother had an idea that she thought would cure me—we would go out in the back yard and ceremoniously "bury the match" as she called it. She and I have joked now for more than 30 years as we recount how she taught me not to mess around with fire by digging a little hole in the ground, tossing in a burning match, and covering it with dirt.

I distinctly remember the day when we went outside to "bury the match," and I distinctly remember playing with fire a million more times after that. In other words, the ceremony didn't work. Ceremonies never do, but faith always does. I never believed that me playing with fire could hurt anyone or burn down the house. I needed to hear the message more than once for any of it to begin making sense.

Faith comes by hearing, not having heard. Hearing comes by the Word that proceeds from the mouth of God right now—not the Word that He spoke thousands of years ago.

"For the Word that God speaks is alive and full of power [making it active, operative, energizing, and effective]; it is sharper than any two-edged sword, penetrating to the dividing line of the breath of life (soul) and [the immortal] spirit, and of joints and marrow [of the deepest parts of our nature], exposing and sifting and analyzing and judging the very thoughts and purposes of the heart."

—Hebrews 4:12

These aren't just black words on white paper or "cunningly devised fables" that we're following in making known the power and coming of our Lord Jesus Christ. The life-breath of God is not some clever story that a bunch of guys sat around a table and came up with thousands of years ago when they said to themselves, "Hey, let's start a new religion and see how many people we can get to buy in."

Jesus says that the words that He speaks are spirit and life, so that if we lay them up in our hearts, they will be the very health and strength of our lives. The flesh profits nothing—it's the Spirit that quickens and makes alive.

Those who live according to the Godless human nature spend life making flesh as comfortable as possible. But we who have received the nature of God welcome and treasure the Spirit above any other love.

> "Whom have I in heaven but thee? and there is none upon earth that I desire beside thee.
>
> My flesh and my heart faileth: but God is the strength of my heart, and my portion for ever."
>
> —Psalm 73:25-26 KJV

The Holy Fire of God should burn just as brightly in us as He does in the very throne room of heaven itself. The Church of Jesus Christ actually bears Father, Son, and Holy Ghost in these ordinary earthen vessels of which our bodily life is composed—"so that the excellency of the power can be shown to be of Him and not of us."[142] As ambassadors from above, we bear the Divine Light, Divine Life, and Divine Love of Jesus the Christ in word and deed as we "aim to bring others into harmony with God."[143]

The fire in us by nature ignites the hearts of those who the Father is in the process of loving into relationship with Him. Yet we're often so consumed with our own lives that the Lord has little opportunity to work in and through us to bring the Spirit to bear in the people that He places around us everyday. At times it's as though the spark of His Presence is buried too deep inside to catch anyone else on fire. In short, we're not combustible enough.

Kind of like the match that I buried in the ground all those years ago, our frail human nature without the Lord sucks the air right out of our ability to burn. The Church has been too caught up in the world's system of being and doing, and consequently our anointing to influence people with the love of God has been compromised.

The Bride of Christ needs once and for all to return to the greatest Truth that we know: anything else that we can attain unto in life apart from God Himself amounts to nothing when compared to the Presence of Father, Son, and Holy Ghost. Husbands, wives, mothers, fathers, sons, daughters, houses, lands—anyone or anything. If all of these lesser loves don't seem like hate in comparison with our desire for Him, then not only have we lost our effectiveness in ministry, and not only have we failed to receive the greatest blessing that He desires to give, but we've also deprived Him of the glory that He deserves.

The Spirit of God moved Paul to say:

"But whatever former things I had that might have been gains to me, I have come to consider as [one combined] loss for Christ's sake.

Yes, furthermore, I count everything as loss compared to the possession of the priceless privilege (the overwhelming preciousness, the surpassing worth, and supreme advantage) of knowing Christ Jesus my Lord and of progressively becoming more deeply and intimately acquainted with Him [of perceiving and recognizing and understanding Him more fully and clearly]. For His sake I have lost everything and

consider it all to be mere rubbish (refuse, dregs), in order
that I may win (gain) Christ (the Anointed One)."

—Philippians 3:7-8

Without Jesus everything else is all just dirt. In fact, Paul
called it "dung"—what he had gained apart from the Lord
Himself. It's amazing how dirt can hold such an illusory sway
over the people of the world—and even the people of God.

For example, think of the value we place on creation,
especially the physical form of the human body. Of course
it's natural to admire the splendor of the natural realm—not
just in people but also in the sun, moon, stars, mountains,
valleys, oceans, etc. The beauty of creation is one thing,
but the majesty of the Creator surpasses everything.

At the end of the age, all that remains will be the new
heavens and the new earth, wherein dwells the righteousness of God—with the Lord Himself as our only Light. As
the Church arises to shake off the dust in which we have
long dwelt, desire to behold the beauty of our Maker above
all else will reign in our lives.

The same chemical elements that are found in earth are
found in man. All the glory of man is like a flower of the field
that fades. Right on down to our very lives without the Lordship of Jesus Christ, it's all just dirt, and we're so wrapped
up in it that it must be appalling to the Holy Ghost.

Remember the disciples, how they admired the beauty
of the buildings of the Temple? Remember how Jesus
responded? "Do you see all these? Truly I tell you, there

will not be left here one stone upon another that will not be thrown down."[144]

It's time for the Church to rise up and come way from operating in the arm of the flesh so that the Lord has constant opportunity to dismantle everything which is not of Him. We've been content to move in the power of another spirit—namely our own. We've operated according to the soulish realm of what seems right to us. We've motivated others with our talents and passions instead of allowing the weightiness of God Almighty to enjoy the place of pre-eminence in our lives and ministries. We've employed eloquent words of human wisdom and devised elaborate building projects which at times are not of Him. In short, we've managed to somehow deprive the cross of power in favor of accomplishing works which are not Spirit driven.

The prayer of Jesus for His Bride is that we rise up and come away from every form of compromise, and return to influencing the world with the Spirit of God.

Not long ago as I reached over to unplug an electric fan and heater in my office, the Lord spoke to me that what I had just done was a prophetic sign for this generation. The Holy Spirit impressed upon my spirit very distinctly that we're not to power the machinery of men any longer by force of personality, intellect, education, or training. Humanity tried that before and it stunk to high heaven. Today, even if we pile up every resource under the sun we still won't do any better.

The Testimony of Jesus

We need the One who has the heavens for His throne and the earth for His footstool to disable all human ingenuity in the Church apart from the Spirit of God—so that instead of operating in the arm of the flesh we return to demonstrating the power of the Holy Ghost. Demonstrating not that we are able, but that He is. Showing forth not our natural capabilities but His supernatural ability to move in power over the entire realm of His kingdom.

When I unplugged the fan and heater that morning, the Lord immediately caused me to remember—He's perfectly capable of bringing the mighty breath of His Spirit to bear without any effort on the part of our flesh whatsoever. God's not looking for a super-human agent when it comes to enkindling a super-human fire in the hearts of men—just an ordinary person who is willing to be set ablaze, get out of the way, and give all of the glory to Him.

Manhandling the Presence of God leads to certain death in the life of any ministry. Just ask Uzza[145] who reached out his hand to steady the Ark when David sought to bring it back again to Jerusalem. More than anything else, we need the fingerprint of God on our lives—our hands made strong by the hands of the Almighty. Us triumphing in the work of His hands, and the beauty of the Lord God upon us—not the other way around.

If we truly operate in the arm of the Spirit of course it will turn people off, but it will also ignite the hearts of those the Lord has called. People aren't necessarily supposed to be attracted; but they are supposed to either be attracted or repelled. No reaction is the worst possible response. Wherever Paul went, the end result was either riot or revival. "To the one we are the savor of life, and to the other we are the smell of doom, a fatal odor."[146]

Beautiful words that tickle the ear will never work if we truly seek to declare the testimony of God. We bear the witness of Him Who was, and is, and is to come. In other words, through our lives and speech we show forth what Jesus has done, is doing, and will do. "And I, brethren, when I came to you, came not with excellency of speech or of wisdom, declaring unto you the testimony of God."[147]

The Spirit of God moved Paul in a determined quest to make knowing Him and making Him known the chief end and aim of his entire life. He understood that if he was to experience the power of the resurrection life of Jesus, then he first had to share a death like His:

> "[For my determined purpose is] that I may know Him [that I may progressively become more deeply and intimately acquainted with Him, perceiving and recognizing and under-standing the wonders of His Person more strongly and more clearly], and that I may in that same way come to know the power outflowing from His resurrection [which it exerts over believers], and that I may so share His sufferings as to be continually transformed [in spirit into His likeness even] to His death, [in the hope]

That if possible I may attain to the [spiritual and moral] resurrection [that lifts me] out from among the dead [even while in the body]."

—Philippians 3:10-11

It's interesting to note that if Jesus had never been crucified, not only would we have never been saved, but He would still be walking around on the earth today. Because the spirit of Jesus had no sin, neither His soul nor body had need of cleansing. On the cross, He accomplished our riddance of guilt, not His own. If not for us He would have never died because death really had no power over Him—not at the very point of dying, not while He was in the tomb, and not ever. It has always been impossible for death to hold Him, and now through the cross we share in His triumph over it also.

Jesus willingly subjected Himself to the pre-determined counsel of the Father so that all things concerning Him could be fulfilled—namely that in Him we would enjoy the eternal life of God. The same life that Jesus enjoyed the whole time He lived on earth.

"The person whose ears are open to My words...has already passed over out of death into life."

—John 5:24

As able ministers of the Spirit, we come heralding the greatest Truth ever known—that whoever believes in Him has eternal life—right now. The blood of Jesus Christ regenerates our immortal spirit forevermore in the very same instant that we repent and place our trust in God. Then the rest of our days on earth are spent with that same blood cleansing our immortal soul as He alone steadily brings us to His goal of perfection. And finally, through the atonement also, God has made provision for an immortal body to awaken out of the dust to be like Him throughout the age to come.

We need a return to preaching "the true words (the genuine and exact declarations) of God."[148] When we worship Him with our whole hearts, the same testimony that He bore becomes ours. The Word we speak gives and brings light, and life, and love because the Word is God, and He is Light, and Life, and Love.

Out of His mouth goes forth a sharp two-edged sword. Out of His mouth we also go. At the sound of His voice, according to what proceeds forth, we're upheld and sustained and refreshed—by every Word. It will always be that our life is in the Son. Just as with the men and women of old, and just like Jesus, we also believe, and therefore have we spoken.

Just like Moses who cried out to God at the Red Sea. And the Lord's response? "Why do you cry out to Me? Lift up your staff (symbol of authority) and divide the waters"[149] so that the entire nation of millions passed through on dry ground in the midst of an ocean. The same Moses who received this testimony of encouragement from God

Almighty—"I will make him (Aaron) your mouth, and you as God."[150]

Just like Joshua who spoke to the sun and moon a word so powerful that even the earth obeyed him and stopped spinning around at 67,000 miles per hour. In commanding the sun to stand still, because of a lack of scientific knowledge Joshua didn't realize that it really never moves. Even so the Lord honored his word and caused the whole earth and moon to quit revolving for an entire day, so that the sun never set as the people of God went out to overcome in battle.[151]

Just like Elijah who said, "There shall neither be dew nor rain these years except by my word."[152] The Spirit of God later recorded through James what we already knew—that Elijah was a man just like us, and yet he prayed earnestly that it might not rain, and neither did it for 3 years.

Just like Gideon who cried out, "The sword of the Lord, and of Gideon."[153] That mighty man of valor instructed the 300 whom the Lord had gathered to each bear a flaming torch in an earthen pitcher and a trumpet in the other hand. When they went out to battle in the strength of the Lord, all of the enemies of His people who were like locusts in the valley for number, fell by the sword as the fire of God exploded in the earth and the trumpet sounded forth like the Voice of God.

Just like Zechariah who recorded this preeminent Truth of God—"Not by might, nor by power, but by my spirit, saith the Lord of Hosts."[154] The same Zechariah who one breath later, still under the unction of the Holy Ghost, encouraged Zerubbabel the priest to cry out to the mountain that obstructed his path by saying: "Who art thou, O great mountain? before Zerubbabel thou shalt become a plain... with shoutings, crying, Grace, grace unto it."[155]

And just like Jesus who charged us to have the faith of God Himself—the very same faith that He operated with during the days of His flesh: "For verily I *say* unto you, That whosoever shall *say* unto this mountain, Be thou removed, and be thou cast into the sea; and shall not doubt in his heart, but shall believe that those things which he *saith* shall come to pass; he shall have whatsoever he *saith*."[156]

If we speak what God says we'll do what He does—namely, rescue and recover people out of the snare of the world, themselves, and the devil. After having given birth to us from above, God sent us back into the earth to snatch other souls from the fire. The only way to accomplish the commission is through ministering the testimony of Jesus Christ, the Word of God made flesh.

"And the servant of the Lord must not strive; but be gentle unto all men, apt to teach, patient,

In meekness instructing those that oppose themselves; if God peradventure will give them repentance to the acknowledging of the truth;

And that they may recover themselves out of the snare of the devil, who are taken captive by him at his will."

—2 Timothy 2:24-26 KJV

The Testimony of Jesus

Not only is the Word the means by which God gathers people into His embrace, but His "mighty word of power" is the creative force "upholding and maintaining and guiding and propelling" the entire universe.[157]

The testimony of Jesus that He has of Our Father is this:

"But as to the Son, He says to Him, Your throne, O God, is forever and ever (to the ages of the ages), and the scepter of Your kingdom is a scepter of absolute righteousness (of justice and straightforwardness).

You have loved righteousness [You have delighted in integrity, virtue, and uprightness in purpose, thought, and action] and You have hated lawlessness (injustice and iniquity). Therefore God, [even] Your God (Godhead), has anointed You with the oil of exultant joy and gladness above and beyond Your companions.

And [further], You, Lord, did lay the foundation of the earth in the beginning, and the heavens are the works of Your hands.

They will perish, but You remain and continue permanently; they will all grow old and wear out like a garment.

Like a mantle [thrown about one's self] You will roll them up, and they will be changed and replaced by others. But You remain the same, and Your years will never end nor come to failure.

Besides, to which of the angels has He ever said, Sit at My right hand [associated with Me in My royal dignity] till I make your enemies a stool for your feet?

Age of the Christ

> Are not the angels all ministering spirits (servants) sent
> out in the service [of God for the assistance] of those who
> are to inherit salvation?"
>
> —Hebrews 1:8-14

The same militant angels that the Father sent to roll away the stone from the tomb of Jesus are at our disposal today. Yet we don't command them—it's the Lord of Hosts who directs the ministering spirits that excel in strength to hearken unto the voice of His Word. As the heirs of salvation we simply partner with them in love as they go forth in power to take away from people their hearts of stone and place within the heart of God.

The heavenly host will accompany and defend us when we act on the promises of God contained in His Word. They perform the counsel of Him who was, and is, and is to come—and He performs the counsel of us, His messengers, when we speak forth on the basis of His Word. It's time to turn loose the testimony of God so that others around us partake of the heavenly calling—for "the Lord is not willing that any should perish, but that all should come to repentance."[158]

When we received Christ as our Savior and Lord, the Holy Ghost enkindled such a super-human fire in the earthen vessels who we are that every single atom of our being is energized by the very life breath of God. Right now we call on the God of Elijah, the One who answers by fire,

140

to burn brighter in the earth than ever before, consuming all that we are with a fervor and holiness never to be extinguished.

10
INDESTRUCTIBLE LIFE

When I was a little kid I remember being fascinated with the idea of a glorified body. I used to always press my mom about giving me some better answers than she was able to provide concerning what I would look like when I got to heaven. It's funny how today my kids ask me the same questions—and I really don't have any better answers.

Actually I have more questions now than ever, but they're the kind that empower—instead of causing doubt to arise they provoke me further into the Presence of God. If we're content with one thing above all else—"to behold the beauty of the Lord and to inquire in His temple,"[159] then all the questions of our minds will eventually be settled forever because the answers are already fixed in heaven.

For instance, one of my goals is to live to 103 so that I will have been married to Elizabeth for 75 years. But just in case, I told her that if I were to ever pass away, I would want her to remarry if she desired. It would be selfish and unfair of me not to release her to love again—as if I alone should enjoy her companionship throughout eternity.

The Lord was asked in Matthew 22, if that were to happen, then "whose wife will she be at the resurrection?"

> "Jesus answered and said unto them, Ye do err, not knowing the scriptures, nor the power of God.
>
> For in the resurrection they neither marry, nor are given in marriage, but are as the angels of God in heaven.
>
> But as touching the resurrection of the dead, have ye not read that which was spoken unto you by God, saying,
>
> I am the God of Abraham, and the God of Isaac, and the God of Jacob? God is not the God of the dead, but of the living."
>
> —Matthew 22:29-33 KJV

Even greater life awaits than what we currently experience—the fullness of salvation that comes only through death—we're "nearer now than when we first believed."[160] On that day when we see the Lord face to face, we'll be just like Him because we'll see Him as He truly is. The Word says that everyone who has that kind of hope in God purifies himself even as He is pure.[161]

The knowledge that one day we'll behold the actual face of God is too much for words, but there's another aspect of the Truth that the Lord sought to communicate in saying, "God is not God of the dead, but of the living."[162]

As the Bride of Christ, nothing, not even death, can

"separate us from the love of God."[163] Even in the earthly realm, God honors and esteems the relationship between husband and wife above all else. Marriage perfectly represents the heart of our union with the Lord—our oneness with Him lasts forever because of what Jesus has done.

Although one day we'll part from this present world, in love Elizabeth took my name instead of keeping her own. In a way the Lord encourages, she and I are too focused on the beauty of our life together to be consumed with the fact that we could somehow experience a brief separation one day.

Actually, that "one day" already came. Our anniversary also marks the day of our death to life apart from one another. When we got married we said goodbye at the same time we said "I do." Goodbye to the way of life that we had previously known prior to committing to love each other for all time.

What happened at the altar on the day of our espousal set the tone for the rest of our life together. Otherworldliness honors God by effectively guarding against the natural human tendency to call things or people our own. Even when our children were born, we immediately offered them back to the Lord as part of the course of our everyday lives.

Love requires no work at all. Personally I've never worked at marriage a day in my life. At the point when we said "I do" then we had a wedding, and so we just keep saying "I do" to actually have a marriage. People always talk about how hard it is and how "you've got to work at it," but love should be as natural as breathing to those who have received the Spirit. We draw upon all that the Lord is and makes available "simply for the self-surrender that accepts the blessing."[164]

The love of the Lord is constant and unfailing, but our experience of His love should always be increasing. If we love God with our whole heart and everyone else the way that we love ourselves, then He promises that blessing will come upon and overtake us.[165]

Notice what the Lord says: *all these blessings will come upon and overtake us.* We don't come upon and overtake them—they come upon and overtake us. Obviously there's such a thing as hard work, but it's based on faithful obedience—and there's always blessing involved—never sorrow. "The blessing of the Lord, it maketh rich, and He addeth no sorrow with it."[166] Perfect rest is our posture before God from which we proceed into the fullest dimension of receiving Him and all that He's made ready for us.

In fact the Word says, "It's vain for you to rise up early, to take rest late, to eat the bread of [anxious] toil, for so He gives [blessings] to His beloved in sleep."[167] In other words, by the Spirit blessings come upon and overtake us in rest—not as a result of our own human effort or righteousness, but according to the goodness of God.

Think of Adam. God caused a deep sleep to come upon him so that when he awoke, he beheld and embraced beauty like He had never known. God wants to do even more in and for us, but somehow just like Adam and Eve later on, we continue to allow wrongdoing to bear down like the weight of the world on our countenance.

When Adam through sin removed Himself from that place of deeply abiding rest in the Lord, the whole race of man fell under the curse of death and hell as a result. Consequently throughout the course of earthly life the Lord said even the ground would be cursed—that in sorrow and toil those bearing the nature of the first man Adam would eat of it all our life—bringing forth bread by the sweat of our brow until we return to the dust from which we came.

Now think of the last Adam—Jesus Christ—the One of whom the Word testifies: "Thy dead men shall live, together with my dead body shall they arise. Awake and sing, ye that dwell in dust: for thy dew is as the dew of herbs, and the earth shall cast out the dead."[168]

Jesus removed our curse by taking it in His own body on the cross. He bore the sin of the world down to hell and left it there—rising to make His victory ours by removing the grave clothes of sin and mire.

> "I am he that liveth, and was dead; and, behold, I am alive for evermore, Amen; and have the keys of hell and of death."
> —Revelation 1:18 KJV

In coming to set us to rights again, Jesus not only restored us, but brought us further than Adam had ever been—all the way to the same origination that He always enjoyed—"I and the Father are one."[169] Our natural bodies were taken from dust and to dust they return, but our spiritual bodies were taken from God by whom we're born again.

Jesus came to place us back in God and God in us—so that just as death had no dominion over Him, neither does it have any rule over us:

> "And if the Spirit of Him Who raised up Jesus from the dead dwells in you, [then] He Who raised up Christ Jesus from the dead will also restore to life your mortal (short-lived, perishable) bodies through His Spirit Who dwells in you."
>
> —Romans 8:11

God's plan for us was never thwarted in the garden, as if anyone or any other force could somehow dismantle the purposes of the Creator for His creation. Although Adam was the zenith of God's handiwork, he was never meant to be more than a type who pre-figured the coming Christ. Through the Lamb who was slain, the Father determined from the foundation of the world to bring us in to the fullness of the Uncreated One—not just to restore unto us the rights and privileges of the first man, no matter how majestic he was.

"The first man Adam became a living being (an individual personality); the last Adam (Christ) became a life-giving Spirit [restoring the dead to life]."[170] Creation and restoration are both works of addition. But restoration surpasses creation in that what Christ has done and will do far exceeds what He originally did. Restoration is not just creation set to rights again—as if that was not enough. No, creation is not only God among us, but Christ in us—"the Hope of [realizing the] glory."[171]

In spirit, soul, and eventually even in our perishable bodies we've been reconstituted in Christ Jesus. The idea in recreation is not just to fix the original or do it again; but to actually surpass the original in every respect. Jesus didn't come to make us like Adam again, and He didn't come just to make us act like Him either. Although we're certainly called to imitate the Lord, He came to do even more by accomplishing the very best in the heart of God—to make us One with Father, Son, and Holy Ghost.

In Adam we found ourselves and lost the Lord. In our lust for self-realization we failed to realize Him—that in His Presence is fullness of joy, at His right hand are pleasures forevermore.[172] But in Christ we've been made alive to the truth that God in us is the greatest promise that we can ever attain. Even a destiny so amazing as having our right to rule and reign forever with God restored, exercising dominion over the whole creation of heaven and earth, is completely superfluous when compared to the Promise of the Fullness of God Himself—personally present in us.

The whole fullness of God lives in the Body of Christ because the same Holy Spirit that the Father exerted in raising Jesus from the death of Adam dwells in us—the

Church. Just as in the beginning God spoke creation into existence, so also Jesus spoke re-creation into being in our hearts. Now the Holy Ghost speaks through us—to also create and restore.

The Word that God speaks through us is full of power. The example of Jesus when He healed and forgave is the same standard of ministry for the Body of Christ today. When the Lord saw a man sick of the palsy lying on his bed He spoke up saying: "Be of good cheer, thy sins be forgiven thee."

Afterward as Jesus perceived the thoughts of the religious people, that they were questioning His authority within themselves, He challenged their wrong thinking:

"And Jesus knowing their thoughts said, Wherefore think ye evil in your hearts? For whether is easier, to say, Thy sins be forgiven thee; or to say, Arise, and walk? But that ye may know that the Son of man hath power on earth to forgive sins, (then saith he to the sick of the palsy,) Arise, take up thy bed, and go unto thine house. And he arose, and departed to his house.

But when the multitudes saw it, they marvelled, and glorified God, which had given such power unto men."

—Matthew 9:4-9 KJV

Jesus extends the same power of the Holy Spirit to each of us who are to inherit the kingdom through this impartation: "Receive ye the Holy Ghost. Whose soever sins ye

remit, they are remitted unto them; and whose soever sins
ye retain, they are retained."[173]

I have a close friend in the Lord who had struggled with
internet pornography and some other lust-related issues. He
came to my house one day asking for ministry according to
the will of God—that if he confess his wrongdoing, the Lord
is faithful to forgive and full of compassionate healing.

As we prayed the Holy Ghost led me to say to my friend,
"On the basis of what Jesus accomplished on the cross,
and on the basis of the promise that He spoke through His
Word, your sins are forgiven."

When my friend heard the truth of that decree, not only
did he experience immediate release from the grip of guilt
and shame, but the weightiness of God Himself was released
in the room to such an extent that it felt like a flood had
overwhelmed us.

Like Jesus we also are son of man *and* son of God, and
we also have power on earth to create and restore. That
the Body of Christ can forgive sins in the place of God probably still sounds like blasphemy to some just as it did in
Jesus time. But if we faithfully herald the truth of what God
has already done, then who can argue with a genuine move
of the Lord?

The Father simply calls the Church to proclaim that in
Christ, He will remember our sin no more—and the Presence of God backs up every Word by shutting the mouth of
whoever rises up in opposition to the Truth.

Age of the Christ

Even so, there's only one mediator between God and man—the Man Christ Jesus. Like Moses who mediated the old covenant between God and the Jews, we represent Jesus who mediated a new covenant to form the new creation we are in Him.

In establishing a people for His own possession, God's dealings in His agreement with Israel were the highest point in His association with humanity since the fall of Adam—until the appearing of Jesus Christ:

> "Who hath saved us, and called us with an holy calling, not according to our works, but according to his own purpose and grace, which was given us in Christ Jesus before the world began,
>
> But is now made manifest by the appearing of our Saviour Jesus Christ, who hath abolished death, and hath brought life and immortality to light through the gospel."
>
> —2 Timothy 1:9-10 KJV

God related to His covenant people of old—Israel—on the basis of the law which was given through Moses. God relates to the new creation who we are by virtue of the grace and truth which come through Jesus Christ. No matter how strongly the Spirit rested upon Moses, like Adam, he was only a type of what God desires for us today. Moses never entered into the promised land, but we who were far off have now been brought near. So near that we are actually One with the eternal Godhead—Father, Son, and Holy Ghost permanently reside in us.

Indestructible Life

Moses was the greatest prophet of God to ever walk the earth until the appearing of Jesus Christ—the one of whom Moses prophesied that the Lord would raise up like unto him. The Word that was spoken expressly by God on the mountain and the mighty acts that the Lord wrought by the hand of Moses were unequalled until Jesus the Christ began to do and to teach the things that form the basis of our faith.

Because he was the meekest man on the earth, God accomplished incredible miracles of power through Moses. Like Jesus, the world itself could probably not contain the books that could be written recounting the mighty acts of God by the hand of Moses.

By lifting up the staff of God to confront the most powerful king on the earth, Moses led approximately three million Jews out of slavery in Egypt. The most famous attesting miracle of the wonder working power of God prior to the resurrection of Jesus Christ happened at the Red Sea where the Lord actually told Moses "lift up your rod, stretch your hand over the sea, and divide it."[174]

On the authority of a single man, the children of Israel—more than three million—went over on dry ground into the desert that they encountered on the other side of the ocean. Instead of the journey into the new land that God had promised taking just a few days as it should have been, for another whole generation Moses wrought miracle after miracle in the midst of incredible opposition to the will of God.

In spite of their unbelief, the entire nation of Israel was miraculously provided for—even walking in divine health for the forty years that they wandered in the wilderness. Finally they were on the very edge of entering in to the promise that God had laid aside for them, but they still complained bitterly instead of trusting in God.

The people were thirsty and seemingly on the verge of destruction, but unlike before when God told Moses to strike the rock so that water would come out, this time He ordered him to just speak to it. But Moses' longsuffering had finally worn thin, and instead of doing explicitly as he had been instructed, Moses struck the rock with the staff of God and cried out, "You rebels! Must we bring water for you out of this rock?"[175] This time the people that God set apart for Himself—a kingdom of priests, and a holy nation—finally drank at the expense of Moses the man of God. He never entered the promised land.

No one and nothing the Lord has placed in our lives should ever be allowed to influence us to remove ourselves from a place of perfect rest in God. Like Moses in that one instance and like the people he led through the wilderness, we too were rebels against the will of God, but the spiritual Rock who followed the Israelites is the same one who pursued us. Jesus Christ, the ever living Son of God, called us with a holy calling into His own embrace, and refreshed us with the fountain of His very life so that we drank the living water of His Presence.

Indestructible Life

Even though Moses died at 120 years of age, "his eye was not dim, nor his natural force abated."[176] The Lord Himself buried the man of God in a valley just outside the land that He gave to the Jews, and no one knows where his tomb is to this day.

Interestingly the Word of God notes later on in Jude 1:9 that the Archangel Michael contended with Satan for the body of Moses and withstood him by saying—"The Lord rebuke thee."

In the power of the Risen Christ, we also dispute with the enemy for the spirit, soul, and body of those around us who have not yet come out of darkness into the marvelous light of God's love. But unlike the archangel Michael, we don't actually have to fight—we just stand still and see the salvation of God prevail in a battle that's already been won. Through our identification with the death, burial, and resurrection of Jesus, the victory that he gained is already ours also to enjoy.

> "Forasmuch then as the children are partakers of flesh and blood, he also himself likewise took part of the same; that through death he might destroy him that had the power of death, that is, the devil."
>
> "And deliver them who through fear of death were all their lifetime subject to bondage."
>
> —Hebrews 2:14-15 KJV

We're more than conquerors through Him who loved us.[177] Prior to the Church of Jesus Christ, there had never been a conqueror on the earth on par with Moses who knew God face to face. Yet we know Him heart to heart. Once we were partakers only of flesh and blood, but now we partake of Christ. Neither the old covenant with the Jews nor the expressions of intimacy and power experienced during the days of the early church are the highest and the best in the heart of God—we are.

Just as we aren't called to return to the days of the old covenant, neither should we hold forth the primitive Church as our standard—no matter how glorious. The Last Days Church is the measure by which we're judged—and "the glory of this latter house shall be greater than of the former, saith the Lord."[178]

The whole cloud of witnesses in heaven surround us here on earth as we all behold "Jesus the author and finisher of our faith; who for the joy that was set before him endured the cross, despising the shame, and is set down at the right hand of the throne of God."[179]

In running the appointed course, the Church of Right Now is called to redeem the time—reclaiming this age by manifesting the fullest possible measure of the stature of Christ. Just like the holy oil which the Lord instructed Moses to compound "after the art of the apothecary"[180] for the anointing of the whole house of God, the fragrance of the Almighty is filling the earth through His Bride who is called to be just like Him—"without spot, blemish, or any such thing."[181]

We took Jesus' Name when we married Him. The Name of the Lord is like ointment poured forth from our lives—a sacred perfume that brings the breath of life to others. Once we were darkness, but now we're light—calling to those who still sleep by saying, "Awake...arise from the dead, and Christ will give you light."[182] The Lord and His Church burning together as One are the Light of the World until that day when we have no more need of the sun, for God Himself shall be our only Light.

His corporate coming lightens the whole earth—we're called to fill the world with the richest measure of Christ. "For as the lightning cometh out of the east, and shineth even unto the west; so shall also the coming of the Son of man be."[183]

No one and nothing can ever contest the glory of the Lord, and no one and nothing can ever separate us from His love—neither "tribulation, distress, persecution, famine, nakedness, peril, or sword."[184]

We overcome by the Blood of the Lamb and the word of our testimony.[185] From a position of resting in His finished work of love, by faith we know that the eternal blood of the Lamb made provision for our perfect well-being. The word of our testimony is the confession of Truth that seals the salvation that He fought for and gained.

"For with the heart man believeth unto righteousness; and with the mouth confession is made unto salvation."

—Romans 10:10 KJV

Having been born again of God we have overcome not only the world but also the wicked one—"and this is the victory...even our faith."[186] The Blood of Jesus Christ protects us from evil and provides for everlasting life. We believe and therefore have we spoken thus—we live under a better covenant based on better promises.

Nothing surpasses what God has done and continues to do in and for and through us who believe. Not the beauty of Adam's original estate prior to the fall, nor the splendor on the face of Moses when God enacted the law. Not even the earthly ministry of Jesus who went on to conquer the grave, nor the acts of the apostles whose faith was attended with astounding miracles of love. But unto us, the Church of Today, God reserves the greatest works of all—and the greatest rewards.

For us who overcome He's preparing a meal of the tree of life in the paradise of God. For us who overcome He's giving hidden manna to eat, and imparting a white stone with a new name written on it that only we know. For us who overcome He's giving the power of a militant love over the nations.

For us who overcome He's giving the Morning Star who is the Son Jesus Christ. For us who overcome He's clothing us all in white—not blotting out our names from the book of life, but confessing us before the Father and the entire host of heaven.

For us who overcome He's making a pillar in the temple of God. Writing upon us the Name of God Himself, and the name of the city of God—the New Jerusalem which comes down out of heaven from the Divine Presence. And not only that, but He's writing upon us His new name—the eternal name of love.

For us who overcome He's granting that we sit with Him *in* His throne—even as He also overcame—and sat down with the Father *in* His throne. The Chief Cornerstone of the Universe will never be removed from His place, and we also will remain in Him forever. The Lord is in His holy temple, seated on His throne. And we are right there with Him, seated with Christ in the heavenly realm.[187]

Our true life is sealed with Christ in God, and from there we descend out of heaven, having His glory—prepared by Him to reign with Him forever and ever. By His own blood, the Ever-Living One purchased our freedom from sin, death, and hell—and gave us the keys of the kingdom instead.

Because the wages of sin is death, Jesus didn't have anything coming to Him. The fact that He lived 30 years on earth without sin prior to His public ministry is as great a miracle as anything He did in the 3 years following. The Lord would still be walking around here on earth today if He had never been crucified, although it's obviously better that He was—not only so that we could be saved from our sin, but also so that He could return to the way He had always been—glorified.

After the Lord's death and burial, resurrection so trans-figured Him that even His closest friends failed to recognize that somehow He was still the same Jesus they had always known—except that the Lamb slain from the foundation of the world now visibly bore in His body the wounds in which the sins of all humanity were hidden.

"The time is coming, and now is, when the dead shall hear the voice of the Son of God: and they that hear shall live."[188] The voice of the Lord so shook the wilderness of our lives that in the heart of God we came out of the tomb at the same time He did.

The Ageless One entered the Holy of Holies once and for all on our behalf, so that we could become the body of believers who represent Him on the earth in every age. Though our spiritual position is one of being seated in the heavens—in a place of resting in what He has done, our work of faith is not finished until the Gospel of the Kingdom is preached among all people throughout the whole world.

God the Father didn't spare His only begotten Son from the pain of suffering for our wrongdoing. Instead He delivered Him up to death on the cross in order to give us opportunity to experience His resurrection life.

Only to the extent that we truly fellowship in His suffering will we also share the power of a new life lived for Him. In other words, if we want His life actively at work in our own, it only happens through the blood of the cross.

As the Body of Christ we are called to be perfectly united and equally yoked with Jesus our Head. In terms of our zeal for the Father, burden for the lost, and brokenness over sin— every aspect of our heart life ought to mirror every facet of His. Jesus Christ is returning for a Bride that's a perfect match in purity, passion, and power—no more and no less.

Not long ago someone told me of a girl he knew that forgot her own name after coming up out of the baptismal waters. That reminds me of what Jesus meant when He said that if we try to save our life then we'll lose it—but if we seek to lose our life for His sake, then we'll find the abundance that He died to provide.

It also reminds me of my own perfect bride who took my name instead of keeping her own, and gave up her life in the Philippines to follow me to the other side of the world. Not knowing where we would go or what we would do, she abandoned all that she had ever loved just to answer the call of my heart to her own. Once she had found the one who her soul desired more than life, every other love was just an afterthought.

"...forget also thine own people, and thy father's house."

—Psalm 45:10 KJV

When I saw Elizabeth Aquino walking down the aisle on the day of our wedding, knowing that she desired me above all and that I loved her as my own life, my heart seemed to almost break the boundary of my chest. At the sound of her "I do" everything within me rejoiced so that I could think of nothing and no one else.

And yet there's a sweetness that we enjoy which surpasses even our life together—the beauty of being enfolded in the arms of Christ forever. Elizabeth and I, however frail we are in this transitory age, will always prefer the Lord Himself above even the chief joy of our own embrace. We go forward settled in the knowledge that throughout the eternity of eternities, what Jesus did in making us One with Him and one another continues on forever...

Now, and in the age to come, as the Bride of Christ our only call is to cleave to Him with our whole heart.

ENDNOTES

CHAPTER 1.....IMMORTAL ORIGIN

1   John 1:13
2   Hebrews 7:3
3   John 8:28
4   1 Peter 2:25
5   Matthew 18:3 NKJV
6   See 2 Corinthians 4:6
7   See Mark 10:14
8   Psalm 8:4 NJKV
9   John 8:58
10   Psalm 90:2
11   Hebrews 1:2
12   Hebrews 1:3
13   See John 1:5
14   John 1:4
15   Hebrews 5:7
16   See 2 Corinthians 3:18
17   Romans 8:18

CHAPTER 2.....BLOOD SONS

18   John 17:10
19   See 2 Samuel 12:25
20   See Luke 16:15
21   Romans 7:24
22   See 2 Timothy 2:10
23   See 1 Peter 2:9
24   John 3:6
25   See Ephesians 2:3
26   Matthew 7:17
27   See Romans 6:5
28   Colossians 1:27

29 Ephesians 1:11
30 John 17:3
31 See John 6:47-56
32 1 Corinthians 6:17

CHAPTER 3.....THE SEED OF GOD

33 Psalm 127:3
34 John 17:21
35 Genesis 1:26 NKJV
36 See Genesis 1
37 1 Corinthians 15:44
38 See Ephesians 3:17
39 Colossians 1:27
40 See Genesis 13:16
41 See Genesis 15:5
42 Genesis 22:17
43 Genesis 22:2
44 John 5:25 NKJV
45 John 12:24
46 See Romans 6:5
47 Romans 4:19-21
48 See Genesis 22:18
49 See 2 Corinthians 4:7
50 See Matthew 17:5
51 See John 14:8-9
52 See 2 Corinthians 3:2-3
53 Revelation 19:10
54 Ecclesiastes 8:4
55 1 Corinthians 3:6
56 Sevenfold ministry of the Holy Spirit referred to in the Amplified Bible in John 14:16,26 John 15:26, & John 16:7
57 See Matthew 12:3-5
58 See 2 Corinthians 5:16
59 Matthew 3:17 KJV
60 Matthew 14:16

CHAPTER 4.....KINGDOM WITHIN, KINGDOM WITHOUT

61 Romans 8:19,23
62 See Luke 13:20-21
63 Galatians 5:9
64 2 Corinthians 5:18
65 Ezekiel 34:16

66 Luke 11:2
67 1 John 4:17
68 Luke 8:22
69 Mark 4:40
70 Mark 4:35-41
71 Matthew 16:19
72 John 20:21
73 See John 21

CHAPTER 5....BETTER COVENANT, BETTER PROMISES

74 John 6:56
75 Romans 4:18
76 See Genesis account of God's dealings with Abraham
77 See Romans 4:21
78 Exodus 34:6
79 John 5:44
80 John 17:22
81 John 10:30
82 Revelation 19:10
83 See 1 Corinthians 6:17
84 See Revelation 1:4, 3:1, 4:5, 5:6
85 1 Corinthians 11:7
86 Colossians 2:9 (emboldened italics mine)

CHAPTER 6....SON OF MAN, SON OF GOD

87 Luke 19:10
88 1 John 3:8
89 2 Corinthians 12:15
90 Matthew 25:40
91 Matthew 25:34
92 Luke 19:10
93 Luke 13:21
94 Luke 19:11
95 See Luke 19:12-13
96 Philippians 2:7 KJV
97 See Psalm 18:35
98 See John 20:21
99 See 1 John 3:8
100 Matthew 10:8 NKJV
101 2 Peter 1:2
102 See Romans 8:35,37
103 2 Corinthians 4:17

CHAPTER 7.....DIFFUSION OF THE HOLY GHOST

104 Ephesians 4:12 KJV
105 Ephesians 4:13
106 Revelation 19:6 NKJV
107 Matthew 12:6 NKJV
108 Colossians 2:9
109 1 Peter 4:10 NKJV
110 See 1 John 3:2
111 See Genesis 2:24
112 See Acts 11:23
113 See 1 John 3:9
114 See 1 Corinthians 6:17
115 See 1 Corinthians 2:13 AMP
116 See Romans 8:32
117 Luke 10:5 KJV
118 1 John 4:17
119 See 2 Corinthians 1:20
120 See Luke 11:2

CHAPTER 8.....THE CHIEF SINGER

121 Genesis 1:26 NKJV
122 See 2 Corinthians 3:18
123 See Hebrews 5:8
124 Luke 9:31 KJV
125 Luke 18:31 KJV
126 Luke 9:27
127 Ephesians 3:20-21
128 See Matthew 17:4, Mark 9:5, & Luke 9:33
129 Matthew 17:5
130 See 2 Peter 1:16
131 See Acts 13:22
132 John 5:44
133 See Genesis 6:2
134 See Genesis 11:6
135 See Isaiah 6:8
136 Job 38:7 KJV
137 Psalm 110:3 KJV
138 Zephaniah 3:17
139 Habakkuk 3:18
140 John 5:25 KJV
141 Habakkuk 3:19 KJV

Endnotes

CHAPTER 9.....TESTIMONY OF JESUS

142 See 2 Corinthians 4:7
143 See 2 Corinthians 5:18 AMP
144 See Matthew 24:2 & Mark 13:2
145 2 Samuel 6:2-7
146 2 Corinthians 2:16
147 2 Corinthians 2:1
148 Revelation 19:9
149 Exodus 14:15-16 (parentheses mine)
150 See Exodus 4:16 (parenthesis mine)
151 See Joshua 10:12-13
152 See 1 Kings 17:1
153 Judges 7:18 KJV
154 Zechariah 4:6 KJV
155 Zechariah 4:7 KJV
156 Mark 11:22 KJV (parenthesis mine)
157 See Hebrews 1:3 AMP
158 2 Peter 3:9 KJV

CHAPTER 10.....INDESTRUCTIBLE LIFE

159 Psalm 27:4 KJV
160 See Romans 13:11
161 See 1 John 3:2-3
162 See Matthew 22:32, Mark 12:26-27, & Luke 20:38
163 Romans 8:39
164 Isaiah 55:1
165 See Deuteronomy 28
166 Proverbs 10:22 KJV
167 Psalm 127:2
168 Isaiah 26:19 KJV
169 John 10:30
170 1 Corinthians 15:45
171 Colossians 1:27
172 See Psalm 16:11
173 John 20:23 KJV
174 See Exodus 14:16
175 Numbers 20:10 KJV
176 Deuteronomy 34:7 KJV
177 See Romans 8:37
178 Haggai 2:9
179 Hebrews 12:2
180 See Exodus 30:25

181 See Ephesians 5:27
182 Ephesians 5:14
183 Matthew 24:27 KJV
184 See Romans 8:35
185 See Revelation 12:11
186 See 1 John 5:4
187 See Revelation 2&3
188 John 5:25

For More Information Contact:

Tommy Green
PO Box 8653
Lexington, KY 40533

www.tommygreen.org

CPSIA information can be obtained at www.ICGtesting.com
Printed in the USA
BVOW06s0727251115

428173BV00009B/73/P